Album of Horses

Album of Horses

By MARGUERITE HENRY

Illustrated by WESLEY DENNIS

RAND McNALLY & COMPANY • Chicago • New York • San Francisco

Dedicated to these horsemen
who drove me on with kindly spurs

ARTHUR C. ANDERSON, harness specialist

COLONEL E. J. BAKER, owner of Greyhound

CHARLES K. BASSETT
Welsh Mountain Pony breeder

WILLIAM B. BELKNAP
Land o' Goshen Farms, Kentucky

ANNE BROWN, secretary-treasurer
Percheron Horse Association

MARSHALL CASSIDY, executive secretary
The Jockey Club, New York

ARNOLD E. CHRISTENSON,

E. F. FOX
American Shire Horse Association

MARGARET CORIDAN, secretary
Clydesdale Breeders' Association

WAYNE DINSMORE, turf consultant

MARGARET DURHAM, Lipizzan fancier

COLONEL HORACE S. FRENCH
Champion of Rex McDonald

DR. FRANCIS HAINES
Co-author, *The Appaloosa Horse*

MR. AND MRS. A. F. HARLIN
Owners of Midnight Sun

ALBERT W. HARRIS, president emeritus,
Arabian Horse Club Registry of America

GEORGE B. HATLEY, secretary
The Appaloosa Horse Club

ANDREW HAXTON, stable foreman
Wilson Six-Horse Clydesdale Team

RAYMOND D. HOLLINGSWORTH, secretary
American Quarter Horse Association

SYD HOUSTON, secretary, Tennessee
Walking Horse Breeders' Association

BEN JONES, trainer, Calumet Farm

KAY AND EVERETT LEDBETTER
Everett Ledbetter Stables

O. J. MITCHELL, Palomino fancier

H. F. MOXLEY, extension specialist
in Animal Husbandry
Michigan State College

DR. WAYNE A. MUNN, president
American Shetland Pony Club

DWIGHT MURPHY, Palomino breeder

W. E. OGILVIE, manager
International Livestock Exposition

COLONEL ALOIS PODHAJSKY
Chief of the Spanish Riding School
Wels, Austria

VERNER L. PUTNAM, trainer

ROY ROGERS, owner of Trigger

FRANK H. SMITH, secretary
Welsh Pony Society of America

SYLVIA MARIA SOUTHARD TIEDTKE
Lipizzan rider

FRANK WATT, secretary
Arabian Horse Club Registry of America

L. B. WESCOTT, secretary-treasurer
American Suffolk Horse Association

BENJAMIN FRANKLIN WHITE
Four-Time Hambletonian Winner

GIBSON WHITE, owner of Rosalind

FLOYD L. WRAY, Walking Horse fancier

and to
these libraries who provided roomy stalls and plump kernels of fact

GAIL BORDEN PUBLIC LIBRARY
Elgin, Illinois

CHICAGO PUBLIC LIBRARY
Chicago, Illinois

THE ALBERTSON PUBLIC LIBRARY
Orlando, Florida

FORT LAUDERDALE PUBLIC LIBRARY
Fort Lauderdale, Florida

Contents

Album of Horses

The Arab

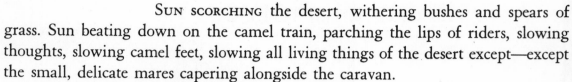

SUN SCORCHING the desert, withering bushes and spears of grass. Sun beating down on the camel train, parching the lips of riders, slowing thoughts, slowing camel feet, slowing all living things of the desert except—except the small, delicate mares capering alongside the caravan.

Silently the cavalcade moves beneath the fierceness of the sun until out of nowhere a cry tears the desert stillness. Sand clouds whirl and hulk along the horizon. An enemy tribe! As one, the riders leap from their camels onto the backs of the mares and gallop toward the enemy, white robes billowing, lances gleaming in the sun.

Now steel meets steel and the mares are no longer playful. They are whirling dervishes—spinning on their hocks, charging, rushing ahead, missing a flying lance, wheeling, stopping, starting, galloping until lungs are fit to burst.

This is tribal warfare. This is Arabia from the ancient days until the time when the deadly lance almost wiped out the fiery little steed.

Always the desert warrior preferred to ride a mare to battle. *Banat er Rih* he called her, which in Arabic means "Daughter of the Wind." And that is how she traveled—a quick gust when the enemy pursued, a steady pace when no one threatened. Endless miles today and tomorrow and the day after tomorrow. And all of this she could endure on the scantiest fare, on dry herbage and bruised dates, and even dead locusts when there were no grasses.

But no matter how meager the fare, her master saw that her thirst was quenched. On the march he carried an animal hide to make into a water vessel especially for her, and at night he milked his camel and gave the fresh, foaming milk to the mare before he fed his family. She was one of his own tentfolk, eating what they ate, dozing when they dozed. Children sometimes slept between her feet, their heads pillowed on her belly.

It is doubtful if the desert men loved their horses as pets. Rather, they depended on them to warn, with loud neighings, of the enemy's approach, to carry them swiftly and safely in battle. And so a good mare was almost never for sale. She

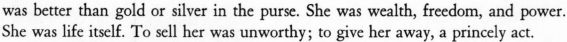

was better than gold or silver in the purse. She was wealth, freedom, and power. She was life itself. To sell her was unworthy; to give her away, a princely act.

An Arab chieftain jealously guarded his mare's reputation for swiftness. And he bred her to only the noblest of stallions so that the pedigree of the foal became sacred. Often it was inscribed on parchment and tied in a little bag around the foal's neck, with a few azure beads to keep away evil spirits.

When a foal was several months old, it was given a camel as nurse-mare. The big clumsy creature adopted the nimble little one wholeheartedly, screaming in worried tones if it strayed, snorting softly when it came near. She refused to move from camp unless the foal accompanied her.

It was common practice to take these foals along on the march, letting them frisk beside their sedate stepmammas. Sometimes during the monotonous journey a young Bedouin boy would spring lightly onto a colt's back, clinging stoutly with naked legs. As simply as that, first training began. Later, as a three-year-old, the colt would be taught the movements of galloping in figure eights, changing leads at every turn, halting in mid-career, and all this was accomplished without punishment of any kind. Horsemen of the desert were patient. They had Time.

To judge the qualities of an Arab horse, the desert men would study the head first. Were the eyes like those of the antelope, set low and wide apart? Enormous and dark in repose? Fiery as sun and stars in excitement? And the ears—did they prick and point inward as if each point were a magnet for the other? And was the face wedge-shaped? Wide at the forehead, tapering to a muzzle so fine the creature might lip water from a tea cup? And did the profile hollow out between forehead and muzzle like the surface of a saucer? If all the answers were yes, the animal was of royal blood.

Color was of no great concern. Chestnut or bay, nutmeg brown or iron gray, all were good. But, under the hair, the skin had to be jet black for protection against the rays of the sun. This underlying blackness is still found in Arabians today and it gives to the bodycoat a lively luster.

As for size, even the smallest Arabians are big enough. Warriors of all eras rode them to battle. George Washington's Arabian charger, Magnolia, was delicately made, but she was big enough to carry him through his fiercest campaigns. And Napoleon's desert stallion, Marengo, bore him on his long retreat from Moscow.

What were the beginnings of these little warriors? Where did they come from? Did the Creator actually take a handful of south wind and say, "I create thee, O Arabian; I give thee flight without wings"?

Storytellers of Arabia explain it this way. "Since time's beginning," they say, "the root or spring of the horse was in the land of the Arab. Our sheiks found them running wild. They caught the foals and gentled them." History can discover no better answer. The Arab horse is the oldest domesticated species in the world. Early rock drawings depict slender horses with arched necks and the typical high-flung tails, for all the world like today's Arabs.

The storytellers relate that the Prophet Mohammed would tolerate only the most obedient mares for his campaigns. To test them he penned a hundred thirst-maddened horses within sight and smell of a clear stream. Turned loose at last, they stampeded for water but, almost there, they heard the notes of the war bugle. Only five mares halted. These were chosen by the Prophet to mother the race.

One of the five was named "Of-the-Cloak" because of a curious incident. A rider, escaping from an enemy, threw off his cloak for greater freedom. Picture his surprise when he arrived in camp to find that the arched tail of his mare had caught and held the cloak. Ever afterward this mare's descendants were called *Abeyan* or "Of-the-Cloak." Today the up-flung tail of the Arab is one of the chief characteristics of the species.

When recent wars threatened the Arabian horse with extinction, Sir Wilfred Blunt and his wife, Lady Anne, imported the finest Arab mares and stallions into England. They knew that Arab blood is a white flame in its purity and, if it were snuffed out, there would be no way to refresh the blood of modern breeds. Today America is helping in the crusade which the Blunts began. There are now more Arabian horses in the United States than in all Arabia! They are used for pleasure and for work on ranches. But these uses are of small importance. Wise horsemen are carrying on the strain, breeding Arabian stallions to Arabian mares to preserve the blood in its purity. Then it will always be available for future generations. Arabian blood is like the rare elements added to steel which give it the superior qualities of fineness and strength.

And so the blood of the "Daughters of the Wind" has streamed west, its strength undiluted, its character unchanged. In the wide-set eyes of these Arabian horses there is still the fire of sun and stars, and in their motion the flow of small winds and the tide of great ones. War horses. Builders of other breeds. Yet holders of their own purity.

The Thoroughbred

A MAN NEEDS SOMEONE to believe in him. A horse has this big need, too. Whether he is bred to race or show-jump or draw a plow, he needs someone who believes in his power to run or jump or pull.

Outward signs of the special qualities of the Thoroughbred may not be visible in colthood. Sometimes the colt is a playboy who resents having to grow up He skitters around his pasture, full of wild notions, and when he is put into training he either throws a tantrum or bobbles along the track from side to side as if he were catching butterflies.

It is then a colt needs championing, needs someone who senses strong fiber and spirit underneath the giddiness. This friend is not always the trainer or owner; sometimes it is the man who rubs, feeds, and waters him—his groom. How that groom tries to get his thoughts through to owner and to trainer! Persistently he corners them and so dead earnest is his talk that the men laugh at the big sounding words and then walk off, pondering the seeds in them. So the colt gets another chance, and another. Then one day he pushes against the wind and opens his nostrils to suck it in. Suddenly he *wants* to run and he does, and he wins! And there at his side, ready with soft warm blanket, ready with words of praise, ready with rub cloths, stands his groom, feeling big in the chest and good.

Everyone whose life touches a Thoroughbred has his own definition of the breed. Man o' War's groom called him "the mostest horse that ever was." Assault's trainer says the Thoroughbred is a creature of bone and blood and bottom. By "bottom" he means stamina and the wind of a fox.

Jockey clubs throughout the world define the Thoroughbred as a running horse whose ancestry may be traced in unbroken line to one of three Oriental sires.

Before these sires were known, there were in England two types of horse— the big lusty steeds used in war, and the small, plain-looking creatures used for the race and the chase. The racers were pony size and pacers mostly. That is, they did not gallop, they paced—the two legs of one side going forward in unison, then the other two.

BYERLY
TURK

DARLEY
ARABIAN

GODOLPHIN
ARABIAN

But when the blood of desert stallions, the blood of the vital little Arabians, began to trickle into England, a curious thing happened. The plain-looking pacers gave way to gallopers, their coarseness was fined down, and the fastest running horse in the world was born.

The three founding fathers of the new breed were the Byerly Turk, the Darley Arabian, and the Godolphin Arabian. The first of the three to appear on the English scene was a tough Turkish charger. Where he came from is mystery. Some say he was one of the spoils of war, and some say his forebears were Arab, not Turk. But no matter. What is known is that he was ridden by a Captain Byerly in King William's War; that he and the captain survived the one big battle in Ireland and returned in fine fettle to England. There, as the Byerly Turk, he sired some famous race horses.

The second of the three was a magnificent bay with a white blaze down his face and three white feet. A traveling merchant named Thomas Darley discovered him in the Syrian desert. By some power of persuasion he did the impossible; he convinced an Arab tribe to sell the stallion. And before the Arabs could change their mind, the handsome bay was bound for Buttercramp in England. Descendants of the Darley Arabian are renowned for their swiftness. One of his great-great-grandsons, well named Eclipse, dimmed the brightness of every other racing horse. He was never beaten, "never had a whip flourished over him or felt the rubbing of a spur—outfooting, outstriding, outlasting every horse that started against him."

In all fairness, however, Darley's Arabian cannot be given full credit for the speed of Eclipse. On his mother's side he was closer to the Godolphin Arabian, the third of the Oriental trio.

The Godolphin Arabian was a little stallion who sired big. His clear bay coat was ticked with gold, and the only white marking was a spot on his off-hind heel, the emblem of swiftness. He was a royal gift from the Sultan of Morocco to the boy king of France, but his deerlike smallness made him the laughingstock of the noblemen. They shunted him out of sight, not caring at all when he was sold to a brutal wood carter. Horse-whipped through the streets of Paris, he was finally bought by a Quaker who shipped him to England, and there he became the favorite stallion of the Earl of Godolphin. Although the fiery little Arabian never started in a race, his name is found today in the pedigree of nearly all race horses.

In Windsor Castle there is a painting of the Godolphin Arabian, and lettered around the frame are these words: "Esteemed one of the best foreign horses ever brought into England. He is allowed to have refreshed the English blood more than any foreign horse ever yet imported."

These then are the three Oriental stallions, the foundation sires of the Thorough-

16

bred. Their blood ran like a fine vein deep through the English stock, strengthening it, fortifying it. And the new breed surpassed both the Arab and the English horses in size and in running speed. Today even the fleetest Arab could not stay with the Thoroughbred on the track.

Has America contributed nothing to the speed of the Thoroughbred? On the contrary, she began early to breed champions. In 1775, Daniel Boone presented to the first Kentucky legislature a bill for improving the breed of horses. Perhaps Squire Boone knew the value of Kentucky's blue grass in building strong bone. Knowingly or unknowingly, he planted the seed that started Kentucky on its way to becoming the land of fine horses.

In style of riding, too, America has contributed to the speed of the Thoroughbred. About 1900, Jockey Tod Sloan made a daring experiment. He shortened his stirrups, moved up from his horse's back, and crouched like a lightning bug on his neck. Here he was so close to the horse's ears he could whisper him home, without whip or spur. Soon all of America's jockeys were riding high, like monkeys on a stick, and their horses were making better time.

This bug-boy crouch not only means more speed but it saves a horse's back, his weak spot. This is important, as many race horses are ridden before they are two years old. Maybe they are not even two, for all Thoroughbreds are given the same birthday, January first. Thus a foal born in April has his first birthday the following New Year's Day, when he is really only eight months old.

Samuel Riddle, owner of Man o' War, used to say that Thoroughbreds have an extra quality greater than speed. He called it heart. "Thoroughbreds don't cry," he would say, and he would tick off on his fingers the ones who showed this courage. There was War Admiral who often limped painfully in his stall. But let the bugle sound and he would walk square and strong to the post and then fight like a gamecock to win.

And Assault, the horse that stepped on a sharp stake, injuring his foot so badly it was malformed the rest of his life. A horse with less heart would have favored it, but he kept testing it, using it, and he became a triple-crown winner, known as the horse that ran on three legs and a heart.

And Black Gold, the middle-aged horse trying for a comeback, who broke his leg in the final furlong but drove on to finish his race just the same.

And there was also the gallant Dark Secret. A sixteenth of a mile from the finish in the Gold Cup Race he ruptured a tendon. Forcing his weight onto his good front foot, he shattered it, too, a step before the line. But he crossed it to win!

No, Thoroughbreds don't cry. Big in heart, high in courage, they go on to finish the race.

The Hunter

WHEN THE AIR is clean and sharp with autumn, then fox hunting swings into action, color, and sound. Consider first the fox, Monsieur Reynard himself. He is a wily, bushy-tailed fellow with traits both good and bad. He kills the farmer's chickens and sneaks his fruit, but on the other hand he also gobbles bugs and grubs and mice. At one time in old England he threatened to become a pest, and the whole countryside was aroused. Rosy-cheeked squires, black-cloaked parsons, butchers, bakers, candlestick makers—all called their hounds, leaped aboard their nags, and galloped uphill and downdale, trying to catch Reynard before he whiffed out of sight into the deep blackness of his den.

As the fox population dwindled, did the Englishmen call off their hunts? No, indeed! The fun grew. They hunted more often. The little red fox was a grand excuse for galloping across country, taking ditches and fences in stride. And whether the sly one got away or there was a kill at the end seemed unimportant. Everyone—horses, hounds, riders—had had such a glowing good time! As for the fox himself, if he escaped he had had the best time of all; he had outfoxed everyone.

In town halls, at coffeehouses, everywhere the talk edged more and more toward fox hunting. It went like this:

"I say, 'tis the hounds that make the chase."

"To *my* mind 'tis the horses—the Irish Thoroughbred Hunters."

"Aye! The beast that can stay the distance and leap like a cat is what makes the hunt, be he all Thoroughbred, all cart horse, or betwixt and between."

Men even talked about dress. Sober homespun coats were well enough, but scarlet coats could liven the landscape. Riders fallen behind would have bright targets to guide them. A clever tailor by the name of Pink tried his hand at cutting and seaming bolts of scarlet cloth, and he did so well in fitting frames both spare and stout that his coats became proper attire and were called "pinks" in his honor.

Along with the new color, spirits soared high. What was once a haphazard fox chase became an organized hunt, with meets held fortnightly.

Often a meet began while stars still pricked holes in the sky, while grass lay drenched in dew, holding the faint oily smell of Monsieur Reynard's prowling footpads. By candlelight men put on their pinks. By lantern light they mounted their stouthearted hunters. Then out they went into the gray mist, heading toward Honey Hill or Squire Higby's place. And just as morning exploded, firing red the maple leaves and barns and pink coats, there they were. All of them: the Master of the Fox Hounds consulting his watch; the Kennel Huntsman, his hounds closely packed around his horse; the two Whippers-In, one ready to scout the fox, the other to round up any hounds that strayed; the Field Master, a little apart from the others, counting noses as it were, taking charge of the big field of mounted followers. There they were, all of them, eager to be off.

A breeze stirs, whetting the excitement. Horses flare their nostrils, hounds look to the Huntsman for a signal, riders take another notch in their girths.

Monsieur Reynard, however, is at ease, licking his chops and lolling in the sun only a little distance from the hunt. He has had a good night of it and his belly is stretched tight with the pickings of Squire Higby's chickens. He lies sprawled on the sunny side of a knoll, protected from the little wind by a boulder and deep woods beyond. Unmindful of the plot against him, he dozes and snores until suddenly he is torn out of his bliss by a single sharp note. The Huntsman's horn! "Run for your life!" it says. "Run for cover! Run!"

Meanwhile the Kennel Huntsman is approaching, signaling the pack, fanning them out. "Leu in!" he cries, and the hounds enter the woods, their sterns upright and joyous. As they begin working to right and to left, a yip of happiness escapes them, as much as to say, "This is our whole life!"

Behind them the Huntsman, the Master, and the followers wait with ears tuned. Many know each hound by voice, by name—the babblers and the dependable ones. The pack is moving ahead now, scouring the covert. Minutes pass, and more minutes, with no sound but leaves and twigs crackling. And then the small sounds are as nothing; one bell-toned hound sings out as she touches the scent. It's Melody's voice!

"Hark!" the Huntsman cries, and he shouts to the pack, "Hark to Melody, hark!" The other hounds move in toward her, noses down tighter than ever. Now she's singing out in earnest, and, one after one, the hounds give tongue until they burst out full of song. All the while the Whipper-In is scouting the open side of the covert, eyes darting, waiting for Reynard to appear. He's up in his stirrups! He sees the fox! With an exultant cry he jerks off his cap and points to the bushy tail streaking across the meadow. "Tally-ho!" he shouts.

And away goes the pack in full cry. The Huntsman lifts his horn, blowing a choppy string of notes. "Gone away! Gone away!" The notes echo and re-echo until the followers know the hounds are on the line and their horses know, too, and they go wild with the chase. Nothing can stop them. Not ditches, nor creeks, nor fallen trees. Up and over them, across miles of country, through meadow and brook.

Only minutes? An hour? Who knows? The scent lost, then found, and lost again while horses take a breather and hounds potter and Reynard leaps onto the top rail of a fence, teetering happily. Does he know his scent has stopped abruptly? He rests a little, then springs to earth for another run. Again the pack gives tongue, and again the earth quakes to the thunder of hoofs. And again the fox baffles his enemies, jumping on the backs of running sheep, wading a shallow stream, back-tracking to the woods, running, running, until at last he can run no more. Breathing deep with weariness he makes a last try for home, his tail dragging over the grass, leaving a strong scent. He can hear the hounds on him, can hear them panting.

And just as they are ready to tear him to pieces, he reaches a side entrance to his den, darts in, and is swallowed by its blackness.

Monsieur Reynard is victor! But strange as it may seem, no one is disappointed —not the hounds nor the horses nor the riders, and least of all the fox. He's had his fun, too, and he will give them another good run some other day.

This is the story of fox hunting—in ancient, tradition-loving England and in young, modern America, too.

After the hunt each horse is walked slowly homeward, then covered with warm blankets. And at night when the rider, too, is under warm blankets and no more than half awake, he takes the jumps again in his mind. He remembers how his mount flew over the widest one—over the stone wall with brush on either side—and he allows to himself that he owns a pretty fair hunter. What if she does have lop ears and turns her toes in? There's Thoroughbred blood in her, Man o' War blood, Godolphin Arabian blood! Perhaps that's why she throws her heart over the jumps and then goes over after it. And just maybe he'll show her this winter with the great jumpers at Madison Square Garden. With a slow finger he writes her name on the bedquilt, Circus Rose . . . . Circus Rose . . . . Circus Rose . . . .

Often the dream spins out to nothing at all, but then again it comes to something. The fox-chasing mare who could jump stone walls did go to New York. Maybe you saw her there, the gray hunter, Circus Rose. She became champion of the year— all because she could "stay the distance and leap like a cat."

And now she's ready for the Olympics, and there will be friends to see her off— huntsmen and hound men, and one among them is sure to call: "Tally-ho, Circus Rose, Tally-ho!"

The Polo Pony

ONCE THERE WAS an English-Irish-American boy with dark unruly hair and earnest gray eyes. He grew up on the marshes of Cape Cod, and his mother wanted him to be a clam digger or an assistant postmaster. Then he could always come home to supper at night and always sleep in his own bed.

His father, you see, just loved to run across fields. He had come to America with an international track team and he had to travel here, there, and everywhere with his team. You can understand why the boy's mother needed one man around the house, even if he was only a teen-ager.

The boy dug clams and painted the picket fence and ran errands and went to school. Then one Saturday afternoon he saw a newsreel in town, and that changed his whole life. Men in white breeches and helmets were whacking a ball as they rode galloping horses. It looked like fun—but the way he said "fun" to his mother over the supper table made it a big word, shot through with speed, excitement, competition.

He asked questions about the game. Did she know how it was played? How *he* could get to play? She shook her head, and the next day the clam diggers shook theirs. They had never heard about a game that looked like hockey on horseback. Only one old man could shed any light on the subject, and this was unpleasant light. "Game's for rich folks, son. Y'got to have a hull string o' ponies. One gets wore out the first chukker. They charge all outdoors for the critters, and good ones is scurcer than hen's teeth."

"What's a chukker, Gramp?"

"I presume likely it's one round o' the game. You got to play so many chukkers to the game. Six, maybe eight, I forget. It takes smart ones to play. Ponies I mean. They can spin on a sixpence and just about guess which way the breakneck fools on their backs want to go."

The boy couldn't put the game out of his head. He just had to hit a ball from the back of a fast horse. He thought and thought how he could make it possible. The summer people on the Cape sometimes kept a horse or two. If he cleaned stables for them, they might let him take one short gallop.

22

He searched and found a family who owned several horses and he worked all the season for them, mucking out stalls, grooming the horses, and finally exercising them. And that fall, when the family went back home, they left one of their horses for him to keep forever, with no strings attached.

From then on the boy never walked anywhere. He rode, five miles to school, five miles home. Then he played polo! Equipment was easy to find—trees for goal posts, a baseball in place of a wooden ball, a hockey stick for a mallet. He bandaged his horse's legs for protection and clipped his mane so that he would feel the lightest touch of the reins on his neck. He taught him to stop suddenly, wheel, and start off at a gallop in the opposite direction. He rode at a dizzy clip and some days he could swoop down and hit that ball—*wham!*—right past the goal. Between games he sponged his pony's face just as the grooms had done in the newsreel and he washed out the horse's mouth. At first the animal reared in surprise; then he enjoyed the cool fresh water and opened his mouth like a bird.

One night the boy rode over to his teacher's house, where he found an old, old book on games. There was just a small piece on polo, but he read it once and then once again until he knew the words:

Historical Summation of the Game of Pulu or Polo

This being a game conducted on horseback with a ball and stick. Designs in early tapestries bespeak evidence of pulu being played in Persia centuries before the coming of Christ; thus no one can doubt its being the most ancient of ball and stick games. An introduction to this wild riding sport was presented to British Hussars in the Punjab by a tribe of Hindu horsemen who raced afield thwacking at a roundish willow root, called a *pulu*. The period for their play was known to them by the Hindu word, *chukker.*

Upon returning to their native heath, the British Hussars continued to have a go at this sport. It has never lost favor, albeit only men of great wealth may pursue its pleasure, requiring as it does a stud of horses so that there may be a fresh one for each chukker.

The game is played in this manner: First, the choosing up of sides, four mounted men to each, then play begins, the object being to drive the ball between the goal posts of the opposing side. Each team acts as a body and the ability of the four players to work together is more effectual than dazzling play by individuals.

There were no pictures at all, so in the margins the boy drew sweeping sketches of horses and Hindus and Hussars and was surprised when the teacher objected.

"Ma!" he shouted, before he went to bed that night, "you *got* to know about this game. It's a team game, Ma. You just support the man with the ball. You ride the opponents off, like interference in football. All you do, Ma, is get the ball through the opponent's goal posts. I've got to get a job and go where I can play polo."

The mother nodded and smiled and gulped down her dreams, letting the words go in one ear and out the other, feeling only the earnestness in them. She knew the boy was little no more. And when the time came, she sent him off to the big city of Boston with her blessing.

He went to work there for a department store, and because he was used to the marsh grass and the sea, he felt boxed-in and lonely. At noon he would draw pictures on packing cases. The manager saw him one day and pushed him right upstairs to draw advertising pictures of men in neat new suits.

The boy turned practically his whole pay check over to the man who stabled his horse, but it was worth it. Visiting polo teams sometimes let him practice with them.

Afterward he would listen to the players talk, the quick-thinking hard-riding men who had records of hitting six, eight, and even ten goals in a game. They told how the great Tommy Hitchcock, the first man to earn a ten-goal rating, started out to practice as a youngster, swinging a stick from the back of a rocking horse; and how later his mother designed a huge wire cage where he and his friends practiced their shots from the back of a dummy horse.

But the talk the boy liked best was about the ponies. He got up courage enough to ask why they were called ponies and he learned it was a courtesy, just as grand-fathers, for example, speak of their white-haired sisters as girls. Those first Hindu horses actually were ponies, and the name hung on even though ponies gradually gave way to the big horses required by big American men.

He learned too that Thoroughbreds crossed with cow ponies made the speediest and handiest mounts. One player said he wouldn't have a pony unless it had first been toughened and seasoned by years of hard and fast riding on the range. The boy noticed that the greater the player, the more credit he gave his ponies. He liked that.

In Boston, too, he joined the National Guard because the army encouraged polo. It made men stronger, braver, better horsemen. Now for the boy there was no more stable cost. The National Guard men played Harvard, and in indoor polo with only six chukkers and a small field the Guard men could hold their own. But the Harvard men had better horses and they won the eight-chukker outdoor games on the big fields. The important thing, however, was not so much the number of goals as the thrill of playing—the speed, excitement, competition.

The boy is man-grown now and he has two polo ponies of his own. He plays with a local team, as hundreds of other men are doing today. No longer is the sport reserved for the men with great strings of ponies. Anyone can play if his heart is set on it.

Only in America could this happen. And it did. The boy's name is Wesley Dennis.

The Morgan

Tony Welling, the mounted policeman, knew he had a good horse in Skippy. But it took a circus fire to prove it to a whole city.

One noonday, in 1942, Tony and Skippy were traveling their regular beat in downtown Cleveland when they saw fire engines racing toward the lake front. Tony put Skippy to a trot and, as they wheeled around a corner in the wake of the engines, a puff of smoke-laden wind struck them full in the face. It came from the circus lot at the foot of the street, and in a quick flash of seeing, Tony singled out the one tent sending up licks of flame. It was the menagerie tent!

In the seconds it took to break through traffic, Tony gauged the fire. Wind coming from the north. The Big Top would be next. Then the horse tent. He began talking to Skippy, thinking all the while of the three things a horse fears— elephants, fire, snakes. "Steady now, Skip. Up the driveway. Past the horse tent. You'll be all right."

The circus lot was mad with confusion. Giraffes and ostriches racing at large; trainers, barkers, clowns trying to capture them. A brave elephant line, marching trunk-to-tail, came so close to Skippy that the burned shreds of their hides brushed his legs. He only shuddered his coat and kept right on toward the menagerie tent.

"Into it, Skip! Into it!" Tony yelled above the screaming of wild animals.

But Skippy was halted by flames. The entrance of the tent was the door to a furnace, and inside the glare only a tiger cage showed clear. A mother tiger, making a fire shield of her body, was trying to protect her cub. All else was ablaze. Tony and Skippy were too late!

Now sparks from the menagerie tent arced over to the Big Top, and with nightmare swiftness the heavy canvas began shriveling like tissue paper. Tony breathed a prayer of thanks that it was too early for the matinee; no children would be inside. He pressed his heels into Skippy's side and urged him toward the horse tent, his voice a mountain of strength.

"Get in there, Skip! That's where we can help!" But could they? The horses,

crazed with fear, were pulling their picket stakes out of the earth, milling around in circles, some dragging the stakes along at the end of their lead ropes. They were stumbling, falling, getting up again, breaking away from the grooms who were vainly trying to lead them out. One man, pointing to a white mare, shouted out: "That one leads the parade!"

Now Tony knew what to do. Cut out the white mare! Lead her away, then hope the others would follow.

"Now, boy!" yelled Tony. "Get her, Skip." Again and again Tony rode Skippy into the bunch, darting this way, that way, trying to outsmart the mare. But she was quicksilver, sliding between the dark horses. Second after second went by while the smoke billowed in, silent, black, deadly. Skippy, sensing the increased danger, hurtled into the mob, threatened the dark horses with bared teeth, got close enough to the mare so that Tony could grab her rope. Tony leaned far out of his saddle, reaching. He had it!

Now for the test. Would the panic-stricken horses follow Skippy with the white mare at heel? They did! As one, the troupe swung into line. But just at the crucial moment of their leaving the tent, a guy wire snapped. It hissed and writhed across Skippy's hoofs.

"Get on!" Tony yelled, impelling him forward with voice and legs. "Get on! It's no snake."

Skippy flinched for only a second. Then, as if he could not show fear before the white mare, he stepped gingerly over the wire and maneuvered his way out through the gate of the circus lot.

Hundreds of spectators lined the exit, and all traffic stopped to let a strange parade go by—a parade of twenty frightened circus horses, without their trappings. At the head of the parade pranced a police horse. His tail and fetlocks were singed and he was shiny with perspiration, but in his eye was a look that told he enjoyed leading the grand spectacle.

Where did Skippy get his bravery? From Tony, of course—through his hands, his voice. But was there something else, too? Some quality far back in his pedigree? Tony thinks there was, and he calls it the Morgan blood.

Skippy was a Morgan horse, and he inherited from the first Morgan his closely coupled body and his sturdiness; but he inherited, too, a great calmness and courage for facing things as they come.

Never before and never since has there been a whole breed named in honor of one horse. And never before or since has there been a whole breed named for one man. For, in this case, both the man and the horse carried the same name.

The man was the frail singing master, Justin Morgan. In the fall of 1795 he journeyed all the long way afoot from Randolph, Vermont, to West Springfield, Massachusetts, to collect a debt. But when he arrived, Farmer Beane who owed the money couldn't pay up in cash; so he gave the singing master a strapping big colt. For good measure he threw in a small one. This undersized colt was a dark bay with black mane and tail, and, in spite of his littleness, his eye was bold and his way of going was big and lively.

The singing master didn't want two more mouths to feed any more than he wanted water in his hat, but two colts were better than nothing at all. "Perchance," he thought, as he led the colts all the way back to Randolph, "I can sell them for the dollars the farmer owed me."

He did sell the big colt, right away, but no one would buy the little one. "Too small," everyone said. Finally he rented the colt to a farmer for a few silver dollars a year. The new master worked him hard—pulling stumps out of the earth, dragging logs, plowing. But, at the end of each day, he was as upheaded and gay as if he had done nothing more than frisk in a pasture. He was ready for anything— even for pulling contests. One night he pulled a log that draft horses and oxen couldn't even budge. He pulled not only the log but three hefty men who sat astride it. He won races, too, from Thoroughbreds. He was draft horse, harness horse, race horse, all in one. He could walk faster, trot faster, run faster, and pull heavier logs than any other horse in Vermont.

When the singing master died, his name was tacked on to the little horse. Justin Morgan, he was called. And his colts and grandcolts, too, became known as Morgans. There was a strange thing about his descendants. Whether they were brown or bay or black, they all had the same round barrel, the same closely coupled body, the same full neck, the same compact look. What was more, they had the same eagerness to go. All-purpose horses, they were called. They helped to pioneer when America was growing up, and they helped to win her wars.

And so the horse that was too little grew to be the foundation sire of the very first American breed. Today, Morgan horses are used by mounted policemen and wherever else a plucky, honest horse is wanted.

Had the singing master lived to see his little colt's descendants, what a stirring song he could have sung about heroes like Skippy!

The Standardbred

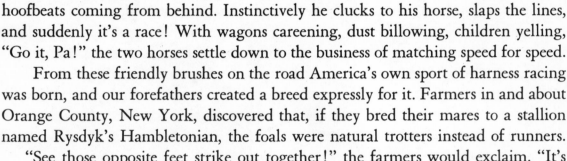

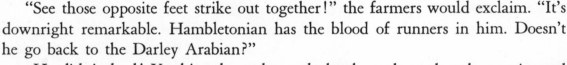

WHEN INDIAN TRAILS through the wilds of America were widened out into roads, then wagons were built and men began to drive as well as to ride their horses. Picture a stalwart pioneer setting off with his family in the go-to-meeting wagon. Driving proudly down the road he helped to build, he hears hoofbeats coming from behind. Instinctively he clucks to his horse, slaps the lines, and suddenly it's a race! With wagons careening, dust billowing, children yelling, "Go it, Pa!" the two horses settle down to the business of matching speed for speed.

From these friendly brushes on the road America's own sport of harness racing was born, and our forefathers created a breed expressly for it. Farmers in and about Orange County, New York, discovered that, if they bred their mares to a stallion named Rysdyk's Hambletonian, the foals were natural trotters instead of runners.

"See those opposite feet strike out together!" the farmers would exclaim. "It's downright remarkable. Hambletonian has the blood of runners in him. Doesn't he go back to the Darley Arabian?"

He did, indeed! Yet his colts and grandcolts showed speed at the trot instead of at the gallop. Today almost all trotters owe their action to Hambletonian's blood, and each year a great race is held in his honor, in the same Orange County where he lived and died.

Upon Hambletonian's death trotting-horse admirers formed a club, and their rules were as American in spirit as the sport itself. Performance, not lineage, was the standard that counted. If a horse could trot the mile in two minutes and a half, or better, he could be registered. This new breed was named Standardbred because each horse had been bred to a standard of speed.

Since then harness-racing parks have sprung up in little and big cities alike. But the homespun country flavor is still there. Instead of flyweight jockeys the drivers are often white-haired substantial men who have bred and trained the horses they race. There is a saying that when breeder-trainer-driver is one man, watch out for a champion!

Such a one was Rosalind. And her famed handicap race brought out a great

courage in the man, Ben White, and in the mare he trained. It is September 9, 1937. At the State Fair in Syracuse, New York, five horses are going to the post in the mile-and-a-half race, the All-American Trotting Handicap. One of the five is Rosalind. As she parades past the grandstand, men of the harness world are aware of her speed. Some watched her set a record in the Junior Kentucky Futurity. Some saw her win the Hambletonian as a three-year-old. Now they have all come to watch her race against the greatest handicap ever asked of a trotter. She must start 240 feet behind the wire, 60 feet behind the nearest horse.

In the faces of the crowd is a look of wondering. Men shake their heads. "It'll take heart, and plenty of it," they say, "to go the distance."

Only one horse in all America would have been penalized more, and that was the mighty Greyhound. Colonel Baker, Greyhound's owner, had refused to enter his horse in the race because he thought too much of the big gelding. "It's an impossible handicap!" he had said. "A horse could spend his heart to win."

Sitting quietly in the sulky, Ben White knows the danger, too. He loves Rosalind. Has he not raised her from a newborn, raised her and her sire and dam, too? But purposefully he drives her out on the track, for he has more at stake than the life of Rosalind. His son's life, too, is at stake. She had been given as a tiny foal to the boy when he was lying ill and lonely in a sanatorium. Her racing pluck had once helped him get well. Maybe, now that he has been stricken a second time, her winning against great odds will help him win his battle, too. It is a chance the father must take.

The horses are heading for their stations: the two bay geldings, Friscomite and Fez, 120 feet behind the wire; Calumet Dilworthy and Lee Hanover, 180 feet. And still farther back—with the greatest penalty of all—Rosalind!

Her driver's eyes are dark and troubled. He is unmindful of the crowded grandstand. He sees only a boy looking bravely out across the desert.

Now it is. Now, on this bright September day, at three o'clock in the afternoon. One o'clock mountain time. Rest time in hospitals. But one boy is not resting. He is holding the lines across the miles.

The father shakes the image from his head, thinking again of Rosalind, his mind on her mind, *in* her mind. He and she have been bred to a standard of speed. This is the time to show it.

Five horses get set on their marks—Rosalind poised for flight, trembling in her eagerness, straining toward the barrier. And now three barriers are sprung at the same instant, and as if some avalanche had let loose, the word "GO" roars from the stands.

Five horses are off! And right at the start Calumet Dilworthy and Lee Hanover move with a rush, passing Fez who breaks into a gallop and is pulled back by his driver, then passing Friscomite.

But Rosalind settles down to business, lengthens her stride. With a stroke of commanding power she reaches for Fez, inches up on him. She catches him and resolutely sweeps around him. Now she's moving up on Friscomite, step by step, and before the first turn she's passing him. And around the turn she matches stride with Calumet Dilworthy, goes eye to eye with him, then trots past him, too. At the quarter-mile pole only Lee Hanover is ahead, only Lee Hanover making it a race.

The father appears calm yet every nerve in his body is alive, every nerve traveling through the lines to Rosalind: "Now, girl, we're about to take the lead. Now we're going out in front." Steadily she gains on Lee Hanover, then skims by him, her stroke fine and square.

She's in the lead at the half-mile! Rosalind with the greatest handicap is on top! Ben White looks at his watch. One minute and ten seconds for the half-mile, with the handicap tucked in. She's taking the track for her own, flying along as if all that anchors her to earth is the sulky and the man sitting quietly in it.

The father's breath comes faster. The longest yards in any race are at the finish. He turns his head to see Lee Hanover coming out of nowhere, making a wild bid for the lead, coming up on Rosalind, gaining, gaining, now pressing her hard.

He reaches for his whip. He has to—a boy is waiting! He taps his beloved filly.

Rosalind feels the flick of the whip, feels the movement of the bit in her mouth. What's wrong? She's gone the mile, yet. . . . The whip? The bit? Hoofbeats thundering hard by? Now she knows. It's *not* over! Lee Hanover is on her, but she won't be overtaken! From deep within comes one mite more of strength, and with a burst of speed she crosses the finish line, a nose in the lead.

Ben White clicks his stop watch. In three minutes, twelve and one-quarter seconds Rosalind has trotted the mile and a half, plus her handicap. She has set a new record for the distance; she has done the impossible.

Smiling, the father accepts the shining trophy, but his mind is busy elsewhere. He has a message to send. "Ten words will do it," he thinks. "Ten flinty, big-going words, big as the mare's twenty-foot stride."

Rosalind wins her handicap race in driving finish. You, son?

The boy won over his handicap, too. He did get well—a second time. And even his doctors agreed that, for him, horse medicine was the best kind of all.

The American Saddle Horse

THE LITTLE OLD MAN shuffled into the grandstand and looked around happily. Sometimes a fellow had to do things on the spur of the moment, like stopping off at the State Fair. Made him feel coltish. It had been a long time since he'd seen a good show for his money. A warm feeling came over him as he opened his program to the same page as the other folks had theirs. He could read the big type without his glasses. SADDLE HORSE DIVISION—OPEN FIVE-GAITED CLASS. He wouldn't bother with the tiny flyspeck type. Didn't know horses or riders any more anyway.

The announcer's voice cut in. "Reverse your horses, please. We will now repeat all five gaits going clockwise of the ring. Trot your horses, please."

The old man let himself be lost in the ring. Bay horses, a gray, sorrel horses with flaxen tails, sorrels with dark tails. And then, flashing from behind, a blue-black stallion—his coat shining like a beetle in the sun.

"Shades of Rex McDonald!" the old man gasped, his eyes fondling the animal as if some dream had suddenly taken form.

He sat bolt upright, his mind leaping across the years. He was a young man, watching a young horse. No! He *was* that horse. That blue-black bullet, prancing around the rings, all over Kentucky, all over Missouri. Walking, trotting, cantering, stepping, racking. He was grand champion of the world. He was Rex McDonald!

Eyes fixed on the black image, he fumbled for gold-rimmed glasses, found them, put them on. Now for a look at the entries' names. Number Seven—Rex Midnight. "The blood is there; *his* blood!"

Bay horses, sorrel horses, horses with white markings. Colors blurred in the old man's eyes like raindrops coming together on a windowpane. How long had they been trotting down there in the ring? One minute? Five minutes? That girl on Number Seven. "Let 'im go, girl. Pick the snaffle to set his head. You're plucking a harpstring, girl. Be delicate fingered."

The announcer's voice was a quick patter in time to the trot. "It's an open class, ladies and gentlemen. Open to horses of all ages, open to all riders."

WALK

TROT

Oldtimer's eyes were everywhere at once, comparing, judging. That sorrel with the flaxen tail. Mostly looks. He felt an elbow in his ribs, heard a young voice say, "Look at that black beauty pop his hocks! He's good fore and aft!"

Pride welled up in the old man. " 'Course he's good. Got Rex McDonald's blood."

"Too bad he's slow, though."

"Slow? He ain't slow! See that sorrel trotting in front and hopping behind? That's what happens when you take 'em on too fast."

Along the rail grooms and owners were crying to the riders as they went by. "Set his head! Take him on! Gather him!"

The old man cried out, too. "Just let him tromp, girl!" But his voice was lost in the boom of the loud-speaker.

"Walk your horses. Let them walk, please."

Twice around the ring. All the horses going airy and bright.

Oldtimer caught snatches of talk around him.

"Only two amateurs riding, the man on the gray and the girl on the black."

"The black won all his junior contests last year."

"Sure he did, but the trainer showed him then. What can a spindling girl do in big competition?"

The old man bristled. "What can she do? She can let her horse do it, that's what." He ran gnarled fingers through his white thatch, remembering when Rex McDonald walked like this, bouncy-like. But his mind was on tiptoe, waiting. Any good Saddlebred could do the natural gaits. The test was yet to come.

"Canter your horses, please. The judge likes rhythm here, not speed, folks."

Impatiently the old man watched the rocking horses down there in the ring, traveling slowly, smooth as a waltz, never speeding up. He took a breath, waiting.

"Walk your horses again, please."

Twice around. All the horses brisk. No one wilting but the old man. He loosened his tie, stuffed it into his pocket, his eyes on the announcer's box.

"Now slow-gait your horses, please."

At last! Here it is! The difficult man-made gait, the gait that leads up to something. The slow motion, the inheld power. The blue-black lifting the left forefoot, holding it poised one split second. Lifting the left hind foot, holding it as if he spurned the earth beneath. Now the right fore high, now the right hind. Up, hesitate; up, hesitate. The girl on Number Seven is smiling. She can feel each beat of the gait. She knows it's right. It's the stepping pace.

The old man laughs out. "Look at that black devil with the angel on his back— she can make him strut in front and squat behind!" He nudges the ribs next to him.

CANTER

36

"Young fellow, see that creature walking uphill on a flat piece of ground? There he is, that blue-black Number Seven."

Suddenly the old man grows fearful. He wants yet dreads the next words. He tries to stay them, but they burst forth splitting the air like a bugle.

"Rack on!"

STEPPING PACE

Bay horses, a gray, sorrel horses. The old man sweeps them all away. Sure. They know the rack is the steppin' pace set to full speed. They can do it. They're all five-gaiters, ain't they? But with the sweat-gleaming black the rack seems not a gait at all. It is a kind of glory. He is scudding clouds instead of tanbark, sailing along, passing other horses as if they did not exist. Suddenly at the turn a sorrel cuts in, almost causing a collision. It's the sorrel ahead now, the black trailing.

But on the straightaway. . . . "By gum, look at Rex pass! He's racking a hole in the ground, leading the whole dang parade!"

The old man is tiring. "Rex can't keep it up forever, judge! Don't you know the strain of it? Tendons ain't pistons, judge. Don't you know it?"

And then, when he can stand it no longer, the loud voice comes to his rescue. "Walk your horses, please. Walk your horses."

A wave of relief washes over the old man. The riders too relax, and the girl gives a saucy flirt of her coattails. He shouts out to her, "Well done, Black Angel!" But he is not alone. The crowd is shouting, too, trying to fill in the eternity of moments while the judge slowly marks his card, slowly steps up to the announcer.

RACK

"Ladies and gentlemen," the voice raps out, "we now have the judge's decision. The blue and the trophy go. . . ."

A lump rises in the old man's throat, but his lips cry the words in unison with the announcer: "—to Number Seven!"

Spent and happy, the little old man puts on his tie, squares his hat on his head, and shuffles down out of the grandstand. What a show he's seen for his money!

That's how it is with Saddlebred horses. They are the world's greatest show horses. Beautiful outside and game inside. Today's Number Seven would lack that touch of greatness had it not been for Rex McDonald and others like him. There are others, you know. But don't let the little old man hear you say so. There's Denmark Number One, foundation sire of the breed. His was Thoroughbred blood and he transmitted his fire to Rex and to the blue-black, too.

The American Saddle Horse, with his refinement of gaits and his animation and beauty, does not belong just to his owner or trainer. He belongs to the show ring, where he can bring joy and thrills to thousands of "ringside riders." He is like a Caruso, like any great artist. He belongs to the wide world—to you and to me and to the little old man crying his lungs out for Number Seven.

The Tennessee Walking Horse

Don't let the name mislead you, for the Tennessee Walking Horse is anything but a heavy-footed nag that can go only a snail's pace. He has, among his three gaits, a running walk as fast and smooth as running water. Because of its gliding motion it gives the rider the sensation of skimming along on a magic carpet.

Thoroughbred champions run the mile in about a minute and a half. Standard-bred champions trot or pace a mile in two minutes. Then, after their race or heats are over, both these champions are through for the day. But the average Tennessee Walking Horse can do the same running walk for several hours at a time, traveling six to eight miles per hour. He is bred not for a flash of speed but for sustained travel, in comfort to his rider and to himself.

What is this contradictory term, the running walk? It is speed from a walk, and actually it is a variation of the trot. Diagonal legs work almost in unison, the left forehoof touching the ground an instant earlier than the right hind. And here is the secret of the speed—the hind foot comes forward well beyond the right front hoofprint, sometimes as much as twenty-four inches! The greater the overstride, the faster and smoother the action.

This running walk is a normal gait for the Walking Horse, and he enters into it with animation. His head nods in timing with his feet, and his ears swing, and sometimes he snaps his teeth so loud they click like castanets. Onlookers often draw back in alarm at the sound, not realizing that the horse is merely swinging to the motion with every muscle he has.

In spite of all this animation the gait is steady enough for a rider to hold a glass of water on the palm of his hand without spilling a drop.

The foundation of the running walk is the slower flatfoot walk with the same trotting action. This is a bold-going gait, straightforward and square on all four corners. And even though the horse's head nods as he steps along, he is far from dozing. He is traveling four or five miles an hour! The nodding is just part of the relaxed rhythm which makes the gait free and easy—to himself and to his rider.

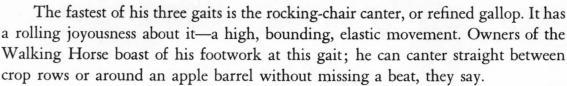

The fastest of his three gaits is the rocking-chair canter, or refined gallop. It has a rolling joyousness about it—a high, bounding, elastic movement. Owners of the Walking Horse boast of his footwork at this gait; he can canter straight between crop rows or around an apple barrel without missing a beat, they say.

For a hundred years or more the Tennessee Walking Horse has been unique in his action and in his services. In early days, when plantations sprawled out to meet sky lines, owners wanted a mount that could easily go forty or fifty miles, day after day. They wanted one with comfortable gaits, with a springiness that would take the jolts for the rider. So, first and foremost, the Walking Horse was a plantation horse; in fact, today he often is called the Plantation Walker.

Circuit riders used the Walking Horse, too. They were the traveling preachers who rode from one little white-spired church to another. Of worldly goods they had none. Their black suits were shiny and threadbare, and sometimes they had no homes at all. But they knew horseflesh as they knew the Bible, and their mounts were the fastest and truest walkers in the countryside. They had to be! Fifty miles to one church, fifty miles to the next. And between the two the road no more than a cowpath—full of gullies and "thank-you ma'ams" and winding creeks that were rivers in floodtime. The circuit horse was a smart one, timing himself to arrive at the little community just when the church bells were pealing. Then he dozed during services, for he had heard the sermon many times before. The preacher, as he rode, would practice his text loud and long. And whether the sermon was hellfire and damnation or green pastures and still waters, always his horse nodded and nodded in approval.

The country doctor, too, rode forth on a Walking Horse, his saddlebag bulging with blue pills and pink pills and bottles and bandages. On dark nights, on muddy roads, through driving rains or gales of wind—he made his calls. In the sickroom ears listened for the familiar running gait, and at the first sound of the one-two, three-four beat, pain and fear began to lift.

What is he, this horse that walks a hole in the wind? What and where were his beginnings? Nearly two hundred years ago adventurous Americans rode over the mountains from Virginia and the Carolinas into Tennessee. They carried their Bible in one hand and their musket in the other—which made them very good riders, indeed, for they must have done all their guiding with knees and heels. The horses they rode were sturdy saddle stock, and a few were Thoroughbreds. The Morgans and the Standardbreds filtered in, too, and soon the middle basin of Tennessee became a melting pot in which four great horse families mingled to make one family. Each breed contributed specific traits, and the result, surprisingly, was a breed with distinctive characteristics. The Thoroughbred family gave strength and stamina, and the Saddlebred comfortable gaits. Hambletonian blood contributed stride. As for the Morgan blood—this gave the Walking Horse his quiet disposition and gentle manners.

In order to have a registry one stallion was selected as a foundation sire. He was Black Allan, and his pedigree is as nice a bit of Americana as one could find. On his father's side he was a great-great-grandson of Rysdyk's Hambletonian, and his mother was a great-great-granddaughter of Justin Morgan. Thus he sprang from two fine American breeds. Maggie Marsh, his mother, was famed in her day as a high-going trotter, and everyone expected her little black son would follow in her hoofprints. He, however, had ideas of his own. He wanted to pace, and pace he did. And so, in disgrace, he was traded in the back country for cows and donkeys. Yet he sired more beautiful and true Walking Horses than any other stallion.

In family albums owners of Tennessee Walking Horses point with pride to their ancestors and the horses they rode. Grandmother sitting sidesaddle on Strolling Jo, her Walking Horse, reins in one hand, basket of eggs in the other, and two grandchildren up behind. Off to town they go, nary an egg cracked, nary a child upset. Grandpa used Strolling Jo, too, for plowing, often teaming him up with some long-eared mule. And teacher, Cousin Kate, rode him to the little red schoolhouse, where as many children climbed aboard as could get seating room. Apparently good-natured Jo had no load limit.

Today, the Walking Horse is by no means limited to Tennessee. The offspring of Black Allan are everywhere. They are today's pleasure horses, the gentle mounts for business and professional people who are not interested in racing over hill and dale on a highstrung horse. For them the running walk or the rocking-chair canter is speed enough. For them the companionship and comfort are pleasure enough. An owner once said that his horse reminded him of a lightning rod, for, as he rode, all the sorrows in his heart flowed down through the splendid muscles of his horse and were grounded in the earth.

Small wonder he thought of his horse as his other self!

The Hackney

THE HACKNEY is a high-stepper. Even going off on a picnic, he lifts his knees and hocks to incredible heights, as if judges' eyes might be peering out at him from every leafy bough. He is born for the show ring, and so inbred is his exaggerated action that he never, never lets down.

Families may forget their own comforts on picnics. Sometimes even spoons and paper cups and a cushion for Mamma are left at home. But the needs of the Hackneys are seldom overlooked. From colthood on they must be pampered because the show ring calls for a fine silky coat and a docked tail.

At the height of the picnic, when children and grownups are slapping at mosquitoes, the Hackneys stand cool and regal in their fly-scrim hoods and sheets. They nibble daintily on the leaves of some tender young tree while an adoring boy and girl shoo away the flies. No sultan on his throne or queen on her couch could have more solicitous attendants.

Docked tails cause extra work for owners and grooms, but the custom is of such long standing that it just goes on. Actually, the tail of a Hackney, if left alone, would be big and bushy, entirely out of keeping with his sleek elegance.

It is an ill wind, however, that blows nobody good, and in at least one instance tail docking helped to make a champion. Captivation was a twitchy, nervous filly with a tail as bushy as a squirrel's. Every time the wind blew, it whipped that tail around her flanks and sent her into a frenzy. She acted as if each individual hair gave off an electric shock. But with her tail docked, and with gentle training, she lost her nervousness and became the darling of the show rings. Whenever the ringmaster began separating the blue ribbon from the others, she would step right out to meet him, knowing she had won.

At Madison Square Garden, at the Chicago International, at all the major shows you see two types of Hackneys, the big bold horses and the dainty little ponies. Both are registered in the same stud book, both are bred for the show ring, and both are built so similarly that the horses look like blown-up pictures of the ponies. Full made they are, stoutly built in proportion to their height, with rather short legs of

immense power. Yet in spite of their robust build, horse and pony both are full of jauntiness and grace. It is no trick at all to find a well-matched pair because many are chestnut or brown with showy white socks. Those socks are washed so frequently that the moment a groom comes in sight with a bucket of suds, up comes a white forefoot.

In England, where the Hackney originated, he was not always this cleanly washed and pampered pet. In the old coaching days he splashed through mud and mire until his white socks must have been a sight. The sorry condition of the roads may have prompted the Hackney to pick his feet high. And his mud-matted tail may have prompted the coachman to dock it.

Before these so-called roads were built, ancestors of the coach horse were ridden instead of driven. Often, besides their stout riders, they had to carry cages of live geese to market and return with farm tools and skipples of salt, not to mention dolls and fripperies. With all these burdens they managed to show speed at the trot. And they were called Old Norfolk Trotters for the county in which they were bred.

The Old Norfolk Trotter was as good and substantial as a loaf of bread. Then horse fanciers decided more yeast was needed. They wanted the loaf to rise higher. And so they mated their good Norfolk mares to the spirited sons of the Darley Arabian. The result was a horse of animation and speed, a lively and high-going stepper. The breed caught on like fire in the wind. In fact, a whole line of descendants was called the Fireaways. America began importing them at once and they became the fashionable park steppers, driven by daring young dandies known as "whips."

The coming of railroads might have put an end to the Hackney's career if, in the spring of 1893, England had not held a magnificent Hackney exhibition. There were Hackneys in hand and Hackneys in harness, and they enthralled the spectators with their powerful action, fore and aft.

Almost from that date on the Hackney was bred for exhibition purposes and he took to his new role with relish. He seemed a born showman, and age only whetted his zeal for the spotlight. At fourteen the famous Cadet Commander displayed as much fire and flash as at his first show. And the judges liked him just as well. In fact, many Hackneys seem to go better with "a little age on them."

Preparation for the show ring takes years. The Hackney's real training begins at the age of three, when many race horses are retired. Day after day, at the end of a long rein, he trots around and around in a great circle. It is months before he is even hooked to a cart and years before he is ready for the ring.

Appearance is almost as important as action, and a Hackney stable is a twenty-four-hour-a-day beauty shop. In every stall, all up and down the aisle, the ponies and horses have their tails done up in tail sets so that they will look very jaunty in the show ring. A pony with heavy jowls is tied up in a jowl strap, much like a lady in a chin strap. The too plump pony wears a leather muzzle over her own to keep her from nibbling between meals. The big Hackney with the leather bib under his chin is a worrier. He worries and picks at his nightcover unless he wears the bib.

Hear the wood rattlers? Those are anklets made of large wooden beads. Of course, the ponies try to kick them off and, in so doing, raise their knees and hocks extremely high. All unknowingly they are tuning up their action.

It is good to know that most Hackneys do not need ankle rattlers. The main part of their action is natural. A colt of six weeks sometimes dances around his mother, knobby knees almost bumping his chin whiskers.

But some youngsters grow lazy as they grow up, and they are the ones that respond to trainers' riggings. With regular sash cord the trainer ties an overshoe on each of the colt's fore hoofs and threads the cord through rings on the bellyband. Presto! He has as fine an action developer as any colt needs.

Now, with the cord slack, out of the stable he goes for his first high-stepping lesson. The trainer clucks softly and, as the colt raises his left leg to step out, he pulls up on the cord with studied care. The colt, without any effort on his part, lifts his leg a tiny fraction higher than normal. The instant he lets his leg down, the trainer releases the cord and then helps to pull the other leg up. Away they go around the ring—for the left foot, pull up, release; for the right, pull up, release. Left; right. Left; right. The lesson is only a few minutes long today. A few minutes more tomorrow.

And then one day the cord is left hanging on its peg in the stable, and now comes the test. The owner and grooms gather around. The trainer tries to cluck as if this day were no different from all the others. The long second. And suddenly the colt starts off. Straight up goes the left foot, twenty inches in the air, then the right its exact twin of motion. Up, down, up, down go the violent little trip hammers. The miracle is complete! Our colt has graduated, and his diploma is a nice long carrot, complete with greens and all.

The trainer's face broadens into a grin, and he heaves a great sigh of relief. In this one moment all the monotony of daily discipline is washed away.

From today on the pattern of high action is impressed upon the colt's mind and muscles forever. But training days are not over. As long as he is traveling the show circuit, a great Hackney, like a great athlete, has to keep in trim—showman and champion to the end.

The Percheron

IN THE BACK YARD of the circus a dappled Gray keeps one ear tuned for the bugle call. The bugle is his clock. It rings an alarm bell inside him, starts off his real day. Soon now; any time now. He listens, grinding his hay slowly, ears pricked. There it is! That sweet brassy discord—*ta ta, ti-ti-ti, ta de, dum dum!*

He lets his wisp of hay fall to the sawdust, then shudders his coat, almost preening. It is his way of saying, "I'm ready." All up and down the horse tent the animals are listening to the stabbing notes. Thoroughbreds are pawing the sawdust, snorting and neighing. But the Gray stands quietly, anticipating the chain of events, each in precisely the right order. At sight of his groom he plants his feet solidly, lowers his head, letting big hands rub rosin on his back, enjoying the feel of long sweeping strokes from withers to tail, again and again.

Next the girthstrap is fastened around his belly, while out in the big tent the band strikes up. Noisy. Throbbing. Brasses wide open, playing the people in. Melody after melody floats out of the big top. Then a lull, and again the bugle! The Gray recognizes his second call. He strides boldly out of his tent, heading for the back door of the big top, almost pulling his groom along.

The show is on! The Grand Spectacle first. Then the waiting for his cue. He nods a little to the music of other acts—a slow tango, a one-step, a mazurka. Now the "Merry-Go-Round" waltz while elephant bulls dance around their pedestals.

This is his cue, this is it! He canters into the center ring, the spotlights following him. And now the band is playing *his* piece! The lilt and rhythm are for him. With a swingy gait he abandons himself to the four-four beat of "Dance, Ballerina, Dance." Around and around the ring he goes. Never changing pace, never faltering, never sensing the peanuts and popcorn and people. Or paper bags crackling or children crying or a stray dog high-tailing it over a tent pin. Not even the pink lady pirouetting on his back! She is no more than a butterfly. For him there is only the roundness of the arena and the same number of paces each lap, around and around and forever around until the melody explodes into a finale, then stops altogether. The dappled Gray stops, too. A moist, slender hand is under his muzzle, as he

46

knew it would be. He licks it slowly, savoring the salty sweetness, while a roar goes up from the crowd and a soft voice tells him he has done his work well.

Then it is over and he is back in the horse tent, having his rosin make-up removed. With a sigh of contentment he reaches down to pick up the wisp of hay he dropped when the bugle sounded.

In the professional world of the circus he is called "Rosinback" because his back and loin are always rubbed with rosin to keep the pink lady from falling off. His color must be either white or gray so the rosin won't show; and his back broad, so it will form a wide landing place; and his disposition calm, for a sudden shy could mean death to the lady in pink.

To the rest of the world he is not a Rosinback at all. He is a Percheron, a big "drafter" who came to America from a tiny district in France.

A small boy played a big part in bringing the Percheron to America. He was Mark Dunham, and he lived in the little village of Wayne, in Illinois. One day in the year 1848, he and his father set off in their high spring buggy for the Farmer's Fair at Springfield. Young Mark, a lad with a lick of red hair and a freckle-dusted nose, fully expected to see high-stepping carriage horses and tough little work horses at the Fair; he was not at all prepared to see as well a deep-bodied animal that had come all the way from France.

He pressed close to the ring where the horses were being shown, and suddenly his breath caught in his throat. The handlers were running into the ring with stallions, and among the small American-born horses he spied a prodigious creature. Different from all others. It wasn't just his bigness, or the fact that he wore more ribbons in his tail and tassels in his mane, or that he trotted as airily as if he were dancing around a Maypole. Or even that he was the one horse that moved in step with the band. It was his *power*. He could crush a man with one hoof, yet he was docile as a pup.

Mark pushed his straw hat back. In all his six years he had never seen a stallion so big and grand. He wished he could pronounce the name Percheron, but the best he could do was shorten it to Perche.

For days afterward, and for years, Mark thought about the wonderful horse at the Fair. And when he grew up, his thoughts amounted to something. He set sail for France and sought out the tiny district of La Perche. There he discovered rolling pastureland with whole meadows of alfalfa and clover. The horses that grazed on it were strong in bone and sinew and muscle. They were every whit as magnificent as his Perche at the county fair. Some were gray and some were shining black. And the finest specimens were branded with two enlaced letters, **P** and **S**, showing they had been approved by the Percheron Society of France.

Mark Dunham asked questions as if he were still a freckle-faced boy. Which color was better? The black? The gray?

The Frenchmen shrugged. The blacks, they explained, were preferred by certain coach drivers of the old days who didn't want to be forever cleaning their horses. The grays were preferred by other drivers because they could be seen in the dark of night and were safer to drive. So Mark Dunham bought some of each, seven in all, and had them shipped to America.

Picture the excitement in the little village of Wayne when a freight train pulls into the station and down the runway come seven horses, weighing a ton apiece!

Mark Dunham is talking to them in French, trying to make them feel at home as he leads them *cloppety-clop* down the lane past the little red schoolhouse and *cloppety-clop* past the little white church. Later, he lined that very lane with elm trees, the same kind he remembered seeing in La Perche, and he planted alfalfa and clover and built red barns like the ones in France. Then he bought more and more Percherons, three and four hundred in some years, until Wayne became the Percheron center of the United States.

Today, the branches of the elm trees he planted meet overhead and interlace like the **P** and the **S** of the Percheron Society. Some of the big red barns are still standing, too. And the descendants of those Percherons are scattered over the United States and Canada. They are plowing, and hauling heavy loads, and trotting to wagon—the power animals of the farm.

Of course, not all are work horses. Some are dapply gray Rosinbacks, awaiting their cues in the back yard of the circus.

The Belgian

SOMETIMES both a man and a horse have a strong sense of determination, and when they put their mind and muscle to the same load, it moves!

Horse-pulling contests at county fairs are as old as kerosene lamps and, like the lamps, they often caused a good deal of smoke. Matched teams took turns pulling a boatlike sled loaded down with stones or sacks of sand. The team that could pull the boat the farthest in one straight pull was hailed champion.

But often such a contest ended in a fist-flying fight. A losing driver would complain that for his team the stoneboat was not set in the same path and the grass wasn't so level as for the winning team. The crowd would split; some took sides with the loser and some rose loudly to the defense of the winner. The fight was on! And it recurred as regularly as harvest.

Finally, after many years of experimenting, a wondrous machine was designed, as different from a stoneboat as a jet plane is different from a kite. It is known as a *dynamometer,* and it has iron weights, like a scale, to register just how many pounds a team can pull. Now, no matter what the terrain—uphill or down, concrete road or cinder path—the resistance of the dynamometer is the same always.

This scientific measuring stick ended the fights of the pulling contests, and it did more. It told the farmer exactly how many pounds his team could pull, and this knowledge kept him from overloading them or making two trips when one would do. But the real and deep benefit was that it acted as a spur in improving the quality of the draft horse. In 1924 the world record was a pull of 3,100 pounds. Now the record set by a handsome pair of Belgians is 4,275 pounds.

Belgians are the big rugged horses that consistently set the heavyweight records. They "get right down and lay right to," as the teamsters say. And so determined are the creatures that onlookers strain forward, tensing their own muscles, pulling as if they were yoked alongside the horses. The field has to be roped off to keep the people from rushing in, and even then they push against the ropes, struggling, straining, sweating with the teams. How they groan if their favorite team falls

short of the goal! And how they whoop and holler when an extra pull sends the register past the two-ton figure!

The driver is not allowed to use his whip, nor even to slap the lines against the horses' rumps. It is the coupling of man and horse that wins. Courage and strength on the part of the horse, coolness and steadiness on the part of the man.

While farmers once had to be wheedled and coaxed and almost pulled in by the ears to hook up their teams to a dynamometer, now as many as 125 pairs are entered in the national pulling contests. In the heavyweight division more Belgian teams compete than all other draft breeds.

Belgians have been asked to go on some strange pulling assignments. Both at the Hialeah race meetings in Miami and at Churchill Downs in Louisville the same four-horse team of Belgians pulls a big starting gate on and off the track. These horses are as beautiful and important in their way as the sleek race horses for whom they work. Shiny chestnut in color, with creamy white tails and manes, they are all pompous dignity. As the runners burst from the starting gate, the four Belgians quiver for just a moment as if they, too, would like to fly around the track. Then they lean into their traces and staunchly pull the gate away, justly proud of their own part in the show.

A study of the build of the Belgian will show why he is a weight puller. His body is compact with great muscular hindquarters to furnish propelling power. And his legs are so short that, when he doubles down into his harness, he seems part of the very earth, almost as if he drew his strength from the core of it. He does not pretend to have high action or an airy way of going; his forte is that strong sense of determination which makes a winner. Stolid, quiet, slow-moving he is, built for big tasks. A wagonload of corn stuck in the mire is a monster rooted until he digs into the earth with his toes and pulls and pulls. A tractor sometimes gives up. "And what's more," says one horseman, "tractors cannot multiply, either; they can only divide and fall to pieces."

Today there are fewer work horses in the United States than there were ten and twenty years ago, but the percentage of Belgians has increased. Not all of them are purebred. Some are grade Belgians; that is, their sires were purebred and their dams were of unknown breeding. But so potent is the blood of the purebred that he stamps his own rugged characteristics on his colts.

What caused the Belgian horse to develop such power? Some think the humid soil which produced the rich grass of his native land helped to build his strong and heavy bones. Belgium is regarded as the homeground of the Great Horse of Flanders, and from him the present-day Belgian is descended. In the Middle Ages, both as war charger and field horse, he played an important role

52

in life. The heavy soil that made him strong required a heavy horse to till it.

The preferred colors have always been chestnut, roan, or bay with flaxen manes and tails. Some of the horses, as they age, grow walrus-shaped mustaches which give them a grave and dignified air.

Although Belgians are a very old breed, they were not brought to the United States until 1885, but almost immediately they were in demand. Farmers discovered that at eighteen months a colt was ready for light work, such as pulling a sleighful of children to school. At two, he could be hitched to a plow, and by the time he was a four-year-old, when other draft breeds were just beginning to work, he was a seasoned veteran in the field.

Belgian owners have a fine appreciation of their breed. Perhaps it takes a man of strong determination to own a horse with the same will. Together, with mind and muscle, they can pull a load out of mud or a farm out of debt.

YOUTH

PRIME
OF LIFE

AGE

The Clydesdale

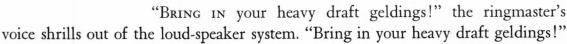

"BRING IN your heavy draft geldings!" the ringmaster's voice shrills out of the loud-speaker system. "Bring in your heavy draft geldings!"

A rustle of expectation ripples over the auditorium. The 4-H boys and girls stir in their seats, eyes darting from one entrance gate to the other.

Suddenly the ringmaster's white gloved hands are raised like ivory batons, and the big drafters come thumping into the ring, each one led by a groom. Ten ponderous animals line up facing the rail, their rolled-up tails toward the center of the ring.

With a nod of his beaver hat the ringmaster tells the judge that all the entries are in. The two wide gates swing shut and there is a heavy pause while the lights stream down on the sleek royal entries, all festooned with rosettes and bows. Excitement mounts as boys and girls, farmers and stockmen lean forward in their squeaking seats, whispering numbers and names to one another.

And now the judge goes to work. With a quick sweep of his eye he looks on the ten magnificent creatures, then points his cane to the one nearest. The groom begins walking the horse in a line straight away from the judge and back again, then trotting him away and back. The judge stops him, picks up a hoof, examines it for soundness, then sends the horse down to the far end of the class.

One after one each mighty animal is studied in action and at place. And now nine are lined up, and a Clydesdale stands alone. He is a handsome bay with flashy white markings, listed on the program as Ferguson's Rob Roy. The judge signals him with his cane, and the groom, looking little and puny by comparison, walks the drafter straight away from the judge. Deliberately the Clydesdale lifts his feet well off the ground, planting his hind feet forward as decisively as his forefeet! The raising and bending action of his hock has the oiled ease of a piece of machinery. A patter of applause breaks out long before the judge is ready to name the winner.

"Reverse!" he barks to the groom. "Trot him back!"

The groom turns the Clydesdale about, and now comes the telling stroke of

the trot. Up to the rail of the ring, back again to the center, working both ways, the Clydesdale demonstrates his ground-covering action while the groom huffs and puffs to keep up.

The people begin clapping to the rhythm. Action! That is what they look for in the Clydesdale. High and lively, so that the flowing feather on the back of the horse's legs makes a big swish as he goes.

The judge's eyes narrow as he looks for more than action. He rocks back on his heels, measuring through squinty eyes. From the top of the Clydesdale's head to the top of his shoulder, from the top of his shoulder to the top of his rump, from the top of his rump to the top of his tail—are these distances nearly equal?

They are! But the judge's face is a mask. He picks up the forehoofs and looks to see if they are bell-shaped and sound. Then, with a wave of his cane, he sends the Clydesdale to the far end.

An utter quiet fills the great auditorium as the judge, without the least haste, walks up and down before the line-up. Then he nods ever so slightly toward the Clydesdale, and the loud-speaker trumpets the words: "First is Number Ten, Ferguson's Rob Roy, owned by . . . ."

But the owner's name is swallowed in the happy din of approval.

Of all the draft horses the Clydesdale is the showman, his long reachy stride covering ground as if he wore seven-league boots.

It is his action and stamina that have made him the long-lived dray horse still to be seen on city streets, but more often in pairs or big hitches on farms all over the world. In Midwest United States and in Canada, in Australia and New Zealand, Clydesdale teams plow and harrow and harvest. And in Argentina in the zone of La Pampa, where the wheatlands flow on and on forever, many farmers use six- or even twelve-horse teams to haul their harvest to the railroads. The long processions look like enormous snakes winding across the land.

These big teams work together as one horse, but each pair has its own job. The leaders, for example, have a little farther to go on turns than the ones behind; so they need to be a shade quicker in their action. The wheel team has to be big and strong because, on a short turn, it is one wheeler that does practically all the pulling. But the swing pair, the ones in the middle, must be as nimble as cats; on short turns it takes quick footwork to keep out of the way of the pole.

If the Clydesdale could talk, he would have a Scotch burr in his voice, for he is the national horse of Scotland. It is good country in Scotland where he was foaled, a country of uplands and lowlands, rich in pasture and in the crops that horses like—oats and hay and apples and turnips. Here, between Glasgow on the north and Gana Hill on the south, the famous Clydesdales were first bred. They took their name from the River Clyde that winds its way through the rolling land. Heavy mists billow into the valley from the Atlantic Ocean, wetting the earth and keeping it always moist. This means a healthy hoof. Today the soundness of feet and legs is one of the chief assets of the Clydesdale.

Some books credit a Scottish nobleman, the sixth duke of Hamilton, with importing six Flemish stallions from England in 1715 to improve the quality of the native Scotch horse. Other history books say it was John Paterson, a farmer of Lochlyoch. But all agree that a black stallion named Blaze had a great influence in establishing the Clydesdale characteristics. He was foaled in 1779 with a wide, white stripe down his face which prompted his name. Perhaps he looked so shiny black because of the contrast made by his white markings. In addition to the white blaze he wore knee-length white stockings. When he trotted, those long white stockings made it appear as if he lifted his feet very high into the air and slapped them down with extraordinary vigor. No one was at all surprised when this action won for him the first prize in the Grass Market Show at Edinburgh.

To most of his descendants Blaze has bequeathed his stylish action and his showy white markings. But his black coat is only occasionally seen. The prevailing colors today are bay and brown.

No one knows who first started the custom of braiding the Clydesdale's mane in an Aberdeen roll. It just seemed to be part of Scotland, like kilts and bagpipes. Instead of plaiting the mane in little pigtails, the Scotsmen started between the horses' ears and braided horizontally along the crest, weaving into it long strands of bright-colored bunting or raffia. This made a roll along the crest but left the remainder of the mane hanging free. To emphasize the arch of the neck, rosebuds on long spikes were fastened at equal distances along the roll and made to stand up like tiny inverted pastebrushes. To this day no Clydesdale ever enters the show ring without having his mane done in an Aberdeen roll.

At the great fairs and stock shows a parade of the prize-winning draft horses of each breed is usually held on the last night of the show. The big powerful drafters prance majestically around the ring, apparently enjoying the spotlight and the applause of the crowd. To the especial delight of the Clydesdale owners, the music by which "the big ones" march is the shrill and windy skirling of the bagpipes! "It's the *verra* instrument," they lean over and whisper to the friend at their elbow. "And see the proud beasts niddin' and noddin' in pleasure!"

The Shire

THE SHIRE is the biggest, broadest horse in the world. He is so big that other drafters seem almost small by comparison. He often grows more than seventeen hands high, and with four inches to a hand his height at the top of his shoulders is nearly six feet. Add to this his heavily crested neck and his strong head, and behold, a creature of heroic proportions!

He weighs a full ton or more. In fact, a 2,300-pound Shire is just a good typical animal with not a bit of fat to spare. He is all bone and brawn and bigness.

Even the feather on his legs is heavy. Instead of growing fine as in the Clydesdale and flowing from the back of the legs only, it tufts out in shaggy abundance all around. Some Shires have long locks of hair growing from their knees as well. It gives them a bold swagger, as if they wore bell-bottom trousers.

In the Shire's native land this feathering served a purpose. His homeground was the marshy fen of Cambridgeshire and Lincolnshire in England. There the land is covered with a rushlike sedge grass, sharp as sword blades, and a horse's heels and legs could be cut as he swished through it. The men of the fenland wear leather gaiters, but horses have to grow their own protection. For many months of the year the fenland oozes with water and bog. Here again the Shire's hairy heels are good insulation; they help to keep the dampness out.

The big husky Shire is a hard worker. He eats up work just as a sawmill eats up logs. Not because he likes to work but because he likes to eat, and he has learned that when his day's work is done he can bury his nose in a box of oats.

In the forests of the New England states and in Wisconsin he drags immense logs to the streams. While the cutting of timber goes on, however, he nods and dozes and peacefully switches at flies. Trees may be felled but the sound of crashing timber barely disturbs his napping, even when the falling log misses his muzzle by no more than a feeler. Nothing much excites him except the *pit-a-pat* of pouring oats. This little sound brings him alive, snorting with explosive pleasure.

Like the Belgian and the Percheron and the Clydesdale, the Shire is descended from the original Great Horse of the Middle Ages, known as the Black Horse of

Flanders. The English people first saw one of these Great Horses when William the Conqueror came riding into Great Britain with a whole army mounted on the huge animals. William the Conqueror, himself, sat a mighty charger that bore him as if he were no more than a puny boy. Actually, William was not only a full-grown man in two hundred pounds of armor, but his horse wore another two hundred pounds besides!

"Here is a stout-hearted beast," the English people exclaimed. "He could be a cart horse as well as a war steed. And we could load our carts to the topmost rail without feeling sorry for the beast." And that is exactly what they did.

For the next span of years they sent to Belgium for the Great Horse, first for one, and then one more, and then many, and they crossed him with their large native mares and produced the Old English Black Horse. In physique he turned out to be even more massive than the war horse.

The new horse was just right, except for his name, Old English Black Horse. This was too long, and his color was more often bay or brown. So he was renamed Shire. Shire is the English word for county, and since the breed was developed in the shires of Lincoln and Cambridge, it seemed fit and proper to call him just that. Now many other shires, such as Kent and Derby and Huntingdon and Leicester, lay claim to the Shire horse, for they, too, are breeding him.

When Henry the Eighth was King of England, he issued a decree that horses less than fifteen hands high should be destroyed. There was not enough pastureland for all, and he wanted to develop a big brawny utility horse. Out of his decree came the real establishment of the Shire breed.

The Shire is as completely English as John Bull. And, appropriately, the name of the first one to be imported into America *was* John Bull. He was as big as his name and twice as powerful, and so well was he liked that a constant stream of Shires was imported during the next fifty years.

Some Americans objected to their heavy feathering, worried about keeping it clean. Yet when the Shire was used to "grade up" the small American horse, that is, when he was bred to American mares, the colts foaled had height and substance, and in many cases the feathering became modest little tufts.

In the cornbelt of the Midwest, farmers have found widespread use for the Shire. And in the Far West, on the great ranches, five- and eight-horse hitches may be seen. Here the Shires work as they did in England, in their slow-moving, powerful way.

How can we tell the Shire from the other drafters? Especially when he often wears the same bay or brown color as the Clydesdale? This is how. We look for size first. Then we look for more subdued markings—a star, perhaps, or a streak

60

SHIRE AND CLYDESDALE

of white down his nose instead of a broad blaze, and white boots instead of long white stockings. We look, too, for the shaggy feather instead of the fine. But most of all we note his mountainous size and bulk.

Everything in any way connected with the Shire is big. The men about him are big, and the carts he draws are big, and the loads and the logs he hauls are big. And a big Shire horseshoe hanging above a barn door, so the English say, is almost certain to invite great good luck.

In the tiny village of Oakham, between the shires of Leicester and Lincoln, there is a quaint custom which goes back hundreds of years. Whenever a noble or peer comes to town, he is expected to hang a horseshoe in the ancient town hall as a token of his visit. The biggest shoes, the people say, bring the biggest luck. And whose are they? The ponderous big Shires', of course!

The Suffolk Punch

In eastern England, between the North Sea and the fens, there is a sunny stretch of land set quite apart from the hurry of the world. It is a land of wide fields and windy skies, and within its boundaries is a kind of peaceful excitement. It is the land of earth artists, the land of the Suffolk man and his Suffolk Punch horse.

When a Suffolk countryman strolls by a tractor-plowed field, he walks unseeing, as if he wore blinders. But a field plowed by a Suffolk Punch—ah, here he stops to let his eye caress the land. He looks across the upturned earth and nods his head at the smoothness of it. Here is the work of artisans! No choppy waves of dirt, but each furrow sliced with such a nicety it seems the hand of God had reached down and neatly combed the land.

The Suffolk Punch belongs to eastern England. He is part of the landscape, part of the economy, part of the history. Merely to look at, he is a satisfaction to the eye. His color is bright chestnut—like a tongue of fire against black field furrows, against green corn blades, against yellow wheat, against blue horizons. Never is he any other color. Of course, the shade may vary up and down the scale from burnt chestnut to bright, but chestnut it must be! Someone once kept a record of twelve thousand Suffolks, and each and every one was a chestnut.

When the wind lifts his forelock, a Suffolk Punch may show a star or a snippet of white on his forehead, and sometimes on his heels there is a touch of white, but often the chestnut bodycoat is so vivid that such markings go unnoticed.

For centuries the Suffolk men have bred Suffolk horses for the fields of Suffolk. Today's farmer may own a tractor, but more than likely he has a Suffolk Punch, too. And his father before him owned a team of Suffolks for every fifty of his acres, and his grandfather before him drove three Suffolks without rein, hitching one ahead of another. And his great-grandfather worked side by side with Suffolks. And so on back for generations the Suffolk man and his chestnut horse together have made eastern England a land rich in grains and grasses.

The Suffolk Punch is the oldest of the draft breeds, and the only reason there

are not more of them in other parts of England and in other parts of the world is that the Suffolk countryman wanted a specialized farm horse for his own farmland. He produced the Suffolk to till his own lands and harvest his own crops, and seldom was there any surplus of horses to sell.

To look at the Suffolk is to know at once he is different from all other draft breeds. He is shorter-legged than the Shire or the Clydesdale, and he has a rounded-up body, a rotund plumpness which the English describe as a "punched-up" look; hence his name, Suffolk Punch. He is not so hairy as the other breeds, either. In fact, there is always a clipped and silky neatness about him as if he had just been groomed.

Other horses would starve and grow gaunt if worked all day long without stopping for the nosebag at noon. But the Suffolk Punch stays sleek and fat on two meals a day—one in the morning and one at night. Between times he goes out to plow or plant or cultivate or mow, depending on the season. And always he walks at a good swinging pace, seemingly enjoying the springiness of the earth. He is not an especially airy walker, but he steps over the nests of skylarks as cautiously as if he knew the treasure they hold.

He can go without eating for a longer period than other horses because he has what the farmers call a bigger "bread basket." That is why he is so valuable to the Suffolk farmer; he can keep right on going until it is too dark to work any more.

Farmers of eastern England will admit that other drafters are "good drawers," but they say that only the Suffolk Punch never gives up. What is truly magnificent about his pulling is that he will get down on his knees and tug and drag until the load moves—or until he drops in exhaustion. And so powerful are his muscles that he can pull on his naked shoulders, without any collar at all.

Where else could the Suffolk farmer find an untiring worker, an easy keeper, and a creature so docile that a little knee-breech lad could manage him?

In this country, in New Jersey, there was once a Suffolk mare imported from the very heart of the Suffolk country. Her name was Finally and she lived up to all the attributes of her breed. She worked the sun up and she worked it down, and she ate her fill only at dawn and dusk. Year after year she appeared in fine fettle and her chestnut coat glistered in the sunlight like water on a millwheel. And year after year she took only a little time out from her work to foal a colt. Even when she was twenty-seven years old, she had a little filly bright as a copper penny and with that characteristic "punched-up" look. Her owners named the foal Finish, and they were proud as punch to think that a mare so old could be so young in spirit and could go on producing such fine children in her own image.

64

The men of Suffolk, however, were not surprised when they heard of Finally's prowess. To them it was only to be expected. Was she not a Suffolk Punch? Did not the Americans know that Suffolk horses are famous for their longevity, that Suffolk mares have colts when they are even ten years older than Finally?

Suffolk countrymen are chary of their praise, and the words of Thomas Crisp of Ufford are a fine example. In advertising his famous Suffolk stallion he said of him: "He is a fine bright chestnut horse standing fifteen and a half hands high, and there is no occasion to say anything more in praise of him."

Yet it is to this very horse of Mr. Crisp's that nearly all Suffolks today go back in direct line. He was the greatest Suffolk of his time, and as Mr. Crisp surmised no one needed to sing his praises.

Suffolk farmers spend so many hours in quiet comradeship with their horses that talk seems wasteful. They could tell you that King George V owned Suffolk horses and "had a capital eye for understanding their character." And they could tell you that the King, like their own fathers, was a Suffolk countryman and that he chose to die within sight of its wide fields and windy skies.

But this, too, is taken for granted. A king rightfully knows that the land of Suffolk holds peace in its loamy goodness and that the place for a Suffolk man or horse to die is in the sun-filled land where he was born.

The Lipizzan

THE LIPIZZAN is a powerfully built animal, yet he is the ballet dancer of the horse kingdom. To the Old World music of gavottes and mazurkas he performs the most difficult routines—springing along on his hind legs without touching ground with his front ones, pirouetting in delicate canter motion, leaping upward into space and, while in the air, kicking out his hind feet. So perfect is his rhythm one would think he had a metronome for a heart!

These leaping, thrusting movements are called courbettes, caprioles, levades, ballotades. Spectators often forget the names, but they never forget the breathless moment when a Lipizzan turns himself into a flying white charger.

Lipizzans are a very old and pure breed. They may be traced back to the year 1565 when Maximilian II, emperor of Austria, decided that his knights needed a riding school like the one he had visited in Spain. The horses trained in it would be beautiful to show in times of peace, and in war they could spring at the foot soldiers of the enemy until they fled in fear. Accordingly Maximilian imported Arabian stallions into Austria and crossed them with Spanish mares. Their descendants became the dazzling white Lipizzans, so named because they were foaled in the little town of Lipizza near the Adriatic Sea.

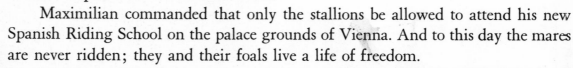

Maximilian commanded that only the stallions be allowed to attend his new Spanish Riding School on the palace grounds of Vienna. And to this day the mares are never ridden; they and their foals live a life of freedom.

Lipizzan colts are a long time growing up. Thoroughbred and Standardbred colts race in public meetings when they are two-year-olds, but Lipizzans run and frolic with their mothers for the first four years of their lives. A pasture dotted with brood mares and foals is a strange sight, the foals dark brown, the mares milk white. Born dark, the youngsters gradually lighten in color, graying at three and becoming pure white by the time they are ten.

Until all the colty foolishness has gone out of them, the young Lipizzans remain at the nursery. Then, at four, they are sent off to school to learn rhythm and manners and acrobatics. Their first lesson is with the lunge rope. Round and round

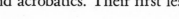

PASSAGE

PIAFFE

LEVADE

in a circle the groom drives his pupil at the end of a long rein. Not until the horse is five years old does he feel a saddle on his back and a bit in his mouth. Then he is walked only, sometimes for months. But what a walk it is! Long, free supple strides, neck reaching out, muscles relaxed. A rhythmic movement.

At six the real training begins, the difficult ballet movements. One movement leads into another naturally, for the rider-trainers are superb teachers. Their commands are spoken in low tones. Their homemade birch whips are cues, not punishing rods. And always their pockets bulge with carrots for good behavior.

When the rider sits his horse, he seems to have a ramrod for a backbone. The fact is that, as an apprentice, he rode for days with an iron bar sewed into the back seam of his riding coat. He appears to sit stone-still; yet he is constantly giving signals. In the *canter,* for example, he sometimes asks his mount to change leads with every stride. If he wishes his horse to take a left lead, he brings back the calf of his right leg, but only a trace. He turns his horse's head toward the left, but only a hair's breadth. He shifts his weight onto his right seat bone. He brings back his left shoulder. But all of these signals are so fine that only the horse is the wiser. Muscle control must be learned by the rider as well as the horse! Small wonder, then, that apprentice grooms start out when only nine or ten and are still learning at sixty-five, even though they are masters. The young apprentice learns most from the fully trained horse, and the green horse from the experienced master. Then, all along the years, trainer and horse continue to learn from each other, growing wise together.

As soon as the canter has become habit, then the stallions are ready for the *quadrille.* In two-four time, to the strains of a Mozart minuet, they are taught to dance in graceful maneuvers. From the quadrille they graduate to the *passage.* This is a slow-to-medium trot which looks as if the feet approach, rather than touch, earth. Diagonal legs strike out in unison, and the action of the forelegs is extremely high. The passage is not spectacular. Rather it is slow, measured beauty.

The *piaffe* next! Piaffe is a French word, meaning to prance. The piaffe is just that—prancing in place, not in stiff movements like a toy soldier, but like a ballet dancer getting ready for an especially intricate routine. In the case of the Lipizzan he is getting ready for the *levade*—the greatest test of a horse's balance. In this exercise he crouches on his hind legs as if he were sitting on his haunches; then slowly he rears until his body reaches a forty-five degree angle, which is far more difficult than if it were held erect. Forelegs tucked under his belly, a thousand pounds of weight poised, he becomes a white stone statue. The best stallions in the school can stand the strain of this pose for no longer than fifteen seconds.

Not all Lipizzans go further in their schooling. Only the very strong can do the *ballotade,* which is a spectacular leap with the hind legs tucked under the belly.

Or the *capriole,* in which the horse springs into the air and, while he is at his highest elevation, thrusts his hind legs out until he is the winged Pegasus come alive.

BALLOTADE

Time and again wars threatened to destroy the Spanish Riding School. In the second World War the Nazis spirited the Lipizzan mares and foals away from Austria and hid them in Czechoslovakia. Meanwhile, at the school, Colonel Alois Podhajsky, chief riding master, tried to save his stallions—rationing their oats and hay, building air-raid shelters for them. But even in the shelters their safety was threatened, for the enemy were moving in closer and closer. Finally the Colonel loaded his pupils on freight cars but could not get them out of the danger zone.

Just when the future looked blackest, U.S. General George S. Patton, Jr., came to the rescue. An expert horseman himself, he asked to see the horses perform. So impressed was he that he wanted to save the breed for future generations. He furnished a convoy of armored tanks to bring the mares and foals back to Austria. And when he was killed, General Mark Clark saw to it that the stallions were escorted to the little town of Wels in the American zone of Austria. Here, on a peaceful, grassy plain, the Spanish Riding School still carries on.

CAPRIOLE

In October, 1950, the same Colonel Podhajsky brought fourteen of his star pupils to America to show the New World the finest horsemanship of the Old. More than a hundred thousand people surged into Madison Square Garden in New York to see the exhibition of the white stallions.

Applause comes easily to Americans but, watching the marbled beauty and the spectacular routines of the Lipizzans, the onlookers sat frozen in admiration. Never before had they seen a horse ballet. The quiet ovation had to come first. Then, like a dike of water unleashed, the applause burst forth.

Before it died away, some horse fans thought, and some said, the stallions must have been severely handled, cruelly treated, to perform so precisely. But how could the casual onlookers know of the long, patient years of training? How could they know that the superb steps are not stunts but that each graceful movement is a copy of high-spirited horses at play or in combat?

And how could they possibly know that, when the white stallions are turned out to grass, they take a busman's holiday? With no audience at all and no riders to cue them, and no music but wind whispers, they spring into a capriole just as boys and girls turn a cartwheel—for the sheer joy it brings!

COURBETTE

The Mustang

HE HAS NEVER LOOKED through a bridle and has never slept in a stable, this half-wild horse of the western plains. His world is the wide open range, the red desert, and the dark hidden folds of the mountains.

His name *mustang* is Spanish for running wild, and he is wild as a tornado—thundering over prairies, zigzagging through foothills, flying along canyon ledges, churning up yellow dust until he is lost in clouds of his own making.

Of all things in life he values most his liberty. Yet his forebears answered the pull of the bit and the prick of the spur. They were the Spanish moor horses and they were brought into Mexico by Captain Cortez. One of the captain's men made a list of them—silver-gray mares, light and dark chestnut stallions, a cream-colored stallion, and a dun with black points. Some he described as being great racers, and some as fast restless creatures, unfit for war.

Perhaps it was these restless spirits that little by little grazed farther and farther away from camp and, suddenly, they were free! The mustangs must have descended from them, for there were no horses in America when Cortez landed. Truant horses from later expeditions joined forces with the first runaways and they all went adventuring together.

The New World was an ocean of grass that billowed on and on until the mountains put an end to it. Here was room to roam—to live like the true wild horses of Asia, the horses that have never been captured. As their numbers grew, they began traveling in bands, each headed by a king stallion who was all powerful. He marshaled his mares, moving them with the seasons—to cool uplands in summer, to warm valleys in winter. He ruled by might, driving and whiplashing his herd until even the little foals ran squealing at his command. But he was wise and brave, scenting danger from afar and protecting his family to the death.

The Spanish invaders, meanwhile, did not miss the few horses that had strayed. They saw that the native Indians could drag great loads, as much or more than a horse. They saw, too, that the Indians trembled and hid behind trees when the white conquerors charged them on fiery steeds.

70

The Spaniards laughed inwardly. A fearful people, they thought, would make good slaves, and they made the Indians into pack animals. But the Indians' eyes were free. They soon discovered that the Spaniards and their horses were not one monster, half man and half horse. They came apart! The Indians watched how their masters mounted and they tried forking their own legs over a horse. Riding was good! In the dark of night they began slipping away from their captors, galloping away with a new prize—a four-legged friend that went on wings of the wind.

Years passed. And more years. And the Indian began to count his wealth, not in pieces of gold as did the Spaniards, but in mustangs. The more he had, the richer he was. And they were free for the taking! He had only to ride the range, round up a wild band, and cut out the particular bullet of horseflesh that struck his fancy. Sometimes this took all day, sometimes all week, but Time for the Indian was not ticks and tocks and alarm bells. He took time by the forelock, as he often did his horse; he was master of both.

The wild bands of mustangs and the Indian tribes loved liberty. Separately and together they roved northward and westward, finally accepting the west for their homeland. They belonged to the wild open ranges, the blue mountains, and the paintbrush flowers. Piebalds and pintos were born to the solid-colored mustangs, and their coats were color camouflage against canyon wall and desert bloom.

When settlers began to move in on the range country, they called the mustangs paint ponies or Indian ponies. Some of the settlers turned out to be as good roundup men as the Indians. They chased the wild bands on horseback, caught a few fillies and colts, and left the others unharmed. It was these mustangs that grew up to develop the west. They were the fast and enduring horses of the Pony Express, the cavalry horses, the cow ponies, the mounts of trader and trapper.

But some were so wild and woolly they could never be tamed, and they became the bucking broncos of the Wild West shows. The moment a bronco felt the scissors grip of a cowboy's legs it drove him mad. With catlike contortions he arched his spine, leaped twisting into the air, and pitched his rider heels over head into the dust. These wild ones often ripped through barbed wire, as if the strands were mere lace, or plunged headlong to their death from high cliffs. They craved freedom more than grass or water. More than life.

Even a mustang broken to the plow often reverted to wildness. In the midst of cutting a furrow he might suddenly break the traces and strike out for freedom, stopping only long enough to let out a great trumpeting neigh. At that commanding ring, gentle old work mares would kick up their heels and follow in joyous obedience. But these raw-boned work mares often lacked the fine heritage of the mustang. Their blood diluted his until the colts and grandcolts were regarded with scorn. "Broomtails!" they were called.

So it is that many ranchers have little sympathy for today's mustang who may be a scrawny creature but who still can fight his weight in wildcats. He fights only as a last resort, however. He prefers to outsmart his enemies, especially the puma who preys on the newborn foals. The moment a stallion scents him he sounds a warning whistle. Quicker than thought the mares bunch the little ones, completely encircle them, and turn their tails on the puma. There they stand motionless, scarcely breathing. The stallion, too, stands still as a rock, but ready to lash out. Seconds go by and the puma slinks off, completely baffled.

But there is one enemy mustangs cannot outsmart. It dives out of the sky, swooping down the mountainsides, roaring over the range, driving the horses hour after hour, giving them no time for a breather, no time to slake their thirst, no time for anything but to run and to run until they can run no more. Suddenly out of nowhere a gate swings shut behind them, and they are trapped in a corral disguised with brush. Only then does the plane fly away, leaving the animals heaving and dripping sweat.

The captured herds serve many purposes. Some of the horses are made into meat, some are used as rodeo buckers, and some are trained to be cow ponies. But always a few escape to be free again, to start life over.

All of these enemies—flying cowboys, wild beasts, the rifles of men—and dwindling pastures, too, are making the mustang a vanishing American. But the Indians on their reservations are harboring the last of the wild horses. The government is willing to give the Indians sheep in place of their little mustangs, but the Indians shake their heads, preferring to be blown along the plains on a wild wind and a wild steed. When the long sleep comes, time enough, they say, to look out on clouds of sheep.

Tourists in the west agree with the Indians. They are not satisfied just to view peaceful hillsides of sheep. They look for live mementos of frontier days. Children especially set their sights high—Indians, buffalo, wild horses! They stand on the brink of canyons, peering down the long reaches. Sometimes all they see is a shimmer of mist. And sometimes they see the outline of a paintbrush pony. It may be only a vision of their imagination growing more and more vivid with their looking. But it may not be a vision at all. Look! A thin swirl of dust! The outline is free flowing, a little broomtail whisking up the rocky wall. A symbol of wildness right out of the past. A symbol of liberty. Of America itself!

The Appaloosa

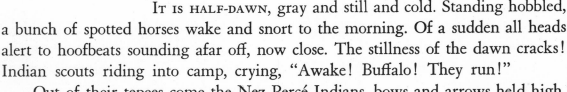

It is half-dawn, gray and still and cold. Standing hobbled, a bunch of spotted horses wake and snort to the morning. Of a sudden all heads alert to hoofbeats sounding afar off, now close. The stillness of the dawn cracks! Indian scouts riding into camp, crying, "Awake! Buffalo! They run!"

Out of their tepees come the Nez Percé Indians, bows and arrows held high. They leap onto their spotted horses and, with eyes fixed on the scouts, take off through a trail winding between trees and brush to a prairie lying deep in shadow.

Buffalo smell is on the wind. And now the shadow divides, breaking up into great lumpy beasts scudding across the mountain meadow. The chase is on! Over wide plains, up and down sharp hillsides, through untracked country the horses charge, closer and closer to the mass of furry beasts. Arrows sing! The dawn is a whirlpool of fury, animals screaming and bellowing, Indians yelling, earth quaking to the thunder of buffalo feet. All along the trail brown hulks fall, thinning out the herd, and after a while the noise dulls and the chase is done.

Full morning comes in a gold blaze, and with it peace to the Indians and the pinch of hunger ended. Buffalo meat is good. The tongue and the fat are delicacies. And the hides will warm the squaws and papooses.

To the spotted horses, too, morning brings reward. Young tender twigs to chew, and time for browsing. Then homeward to the sheltered valley of the Winding Waters.

Of all the Indian tribes in Northwest America the Nez Percés were the wisest horsemen. As a squaw sorts berries, they sorted and culled their horses. The poorer ones were traded off or used as pack horses, the gentle aged ones became mounts for the old people. But the swift ones, the tough and game ones—these were the buffalo runners and they had no equal. They could travel the craggy mountains at full gallop. They could charge into stampeding buffalo and single out one for the kill. They were built for rough terrain: forefeet turned in so they could toe-dance the narrowest passes; wide heels to make them sure-footed; thin tails that whisked through brush and brier without being caught.

Other tribes painted their horses for war and for the chase. But the Nez Percé horses were painted by nature with a curious spattering of spots in clay-red or jet black. Some spots were rounded like polka dots, some irregular as leaves, and some elongated like footprints.

What did it matter that the hostile Blackfeet tribe had guns with flint stones? The spotted horses could outmaneuver their guns and outrun their mounts.

And so the Nez Percés lived in security—migrating and hunting by horse, and breeding only the best to the best until, in time, their horses were the most distinctive in marking and the fleetest of foot in the Pacific Northwest.

When white men spied them, they said, "These are the swift runners that graze on the meadows made by the Palouse River." Soon the word Palouse, which means "the stream of the green meadows," came to apply to the horses, too. "Palouseys," they were called. Even the Indians began speaking of their red and blue Palouseys, for most of them were red or blue roans, whitening toward the rump where the spots clustered.

The Indians took a liking to the white-faced men. They invited them to feast on buffalo meat and wild thimbleberries. And they gave them presents of horses. The white men in turn sent missionaries to live among the Indians to teach them reading and writing. The missionaries disapproved of the fast spotted horses and of the constant warfare with the Blackfeet. So they showed the Nez Percés how to make plows and cultivate the land. And they gave them Bible names, calling their elderly chieftain Joseph and changing the name of his son from "Thunder Rolling in the Mountains" to "Young Joseph."

Quiet years followed, in which the spotted horses worked the rich soil of the valley. Then in 1860 a nugget of gold was discovered, and seemingly from nowhere came a stampede of men—gold rushers who trampled vegetable patches and despoiled pastureland. Settlers came, too, jostling the red man, squatting on his land, eyeing his cattle and his horses.

Meanwhile, far away in the capital city of the United States, greedy fingers pointed across the continent and voices blustered: "We must move the Nez Percés to a reservation." Agents came to the valley, saying, "This spot is now too cold for you. You must go away to Idaho."

Young Joseph was now chief of his tribe. He listened, puzzled. By solemn treaty his people had been given the valley of the Winding Waters, the Wallowa Valley of Oregon. "Words, words," he said to the agents. "With a forked tongue the white man makes promises. The words come to nothing."

For answer soldiers moved into the valley and drove the Indians out. Bewildered, they rounded up their horses and tried to swim them across the Snake River.

It was floodtime and many animals were drowned. Those left on the banks were stolen by the white soldiers and their guards killed.

Young Joseph had tried to keep his tribesmen from going on the warpath, but now his blood was on fire, too. He became again Chief Thunder Rolling in the Mountains, and his fighting bore fierce testimony to his name. Outnumbered ten to one, he and his small band defeated three armies within sixty days! And always the Indians had their families, and household goods, and remnants of their cattle to worry them. Their only allies were the spotted horses.

Three times they crossed the Continental Divide only to find that the white generals had endless resources of troops. At last, after a flight of a thousand miles, Chief Thunder Rolling in the Mountains surrendered. "From where the sun now stands," he said, "we will fight no more forever." And they never have.

Their surviving horses were taken away and sold until they became an almost forgotten breed. The last words of Joseph were: "We gave up all our horses, and we have not heard of them since. *Somebody has got our horses.*"

Time fell away. Days and years passed. In 1937 Francis Haines, a student in Idaho, was poking and prying into the history of the Nez Percé Indians. In the midst of his searching he suddenly became aware that the horses of the Nez Percés were running away with his thoughts. He began digging deeper into the past and discovered that twenty centuries ago the Appaloosas were known in China as the heavenly horses and in Persia as the sacred horses. Through wars and conquests he traced them from Asia to Spain to Mexico to the Pacific Northwest.

Could he stand by and let a breed that had survived wars and centuries die out? He sat down at his typewriter and pounded out words that had a sting to them. They roused horsemen who scoured the valleys and plains and mountain hideouts. They found a few of the spotted horses, and, once again, horsemen began to sort and cull and breed only the best to the best. Today the almost lost breed is 1,400 strong. They are no longer buffalo runners; they are the range horses of the cattle country.

And what of the gallant Nez Percés? Their descendants are now living quietly and peaceably on the Lapwai Reservation. One day a year, at the National Appaloosa Show, a young brave is sometimes asked to mount a red or blue "Palousey" decorated with the saddle pad and bridle once belonging to Chief Thunder Rolling in the Mountains. Then a strong and joyous feeling comes over the spectators, white and Indian alike. It is almost as if the Chieftain had come alive to speak for his people: "Our spotted breed is on the comeback trail. The white scholar of Idaho spoke with a straight tongue; *his* words came to something."

The Quarter Horse

He is not a quarter of a horse or a quarter of anything. He is himself—the fastest piece of horseflesh in the world for a quarter of a mile. Hence his name, a name he has borne almost since the first colonists landed in Virginia.

Long before the American Revolution, long before the creation of the Thoroughbred, the Quarter Horse was an old established strain. He was bred for two purposes, to work and to race, and he excelled at both. On work days he chased wild cattle—rounding them up, driving them into the cowpens. But on holidays he was a race horse.

There were no smooth oval tracks in those days, only straightaways carved out of virgin forests. Occasionally the path was so rough that men used their wives' big iron kettles, turned upside down, to scrape it smooth. Sometimes this racing strip was only ten yards long and sometimes it stretched out the full quarter of a mile but, whatever the distance, the colonists reveled in the quick flash of speed. It lifted their weariness, relaxed muscles aching from the work of settling a new land, dulled the homesickness for the land they had left.

It took only two horses to make a race and any clearing to make a track. Owners made the best jockeys. With pantaloons bellying in the wind and kerchiefs tying down their hair they urged their chunky steeds to victory. All along the race path white men in coonskin caps, red men in feather headdress, Quakers in sober black, cavaliers in their old finery—all shouted as one man, throwing assorted headgear into the air for the winner.

The Indians who came to watch were friendly. They rode in from the backwoods on little Spanish mustangs, bringing an extra one or two to trade for tobacco or beads. It was easy to find a trader, for the colonists liked this wiry animal. It was the mustang who had contributed speed to their Quarter Horses! The first settlers had bred their stout-bodied English horses to him and in this way had developed a short-legged running horse of great strength and swiftness.

The Quarter Horses were the first race horses of America, and they became so

famous that men referred to them by their initials alone. In early books, in letters and diaries, they wrote of their C.A.Q.R.H., meaning their Celebrated American Quarter Running Horses. They described them as being "not very tall, but hardy, strong, and fleet."

For nearly a hundred years the C.A.Q.R.H. were the only race horses in America. Then, on sailing ships from England, came the Thoroughbred. And, with his coming, the scene changed. Race courses were built, a whole mile long. Flyweight jockeys were hired, and they wore bright silk jackets and jockey caps, instead of pantaloons and kerchiefs.

It was inevitable that the short-legged Quarter Horse and the long-legged Thoroughbred should be matched on the new race courses. And results, too, were inevitable. The Quarter Horse jumped away from the starting point and led to the first quarter. Then the Thoroughbred came on to win.

The Thoroughbred was built for sustained speed. Everything about him was long and rangy—long legs, long body, long neck, even his ears grew longer than those of the Quarter Horse. He was built exactly like a greyhound and he stretched out in his going like a greyhound. Pound for pound the Thoroughbred and the Quarter Horse weighed the same. But there the resemblance ended. It was a case of greyhound versus bulldog.

The Quarter Horse was short-legged, short-backed, short-necked—even his ears were short. Little fox ears they were called. Alongside him the Thoroughbred seemed almost gaunt, for the Quarter Horse was bunched with muscle. His chest, his shoulder, his forearm, his hind quarters bulged with layers of muscle. His jaw, too, was muscled and massive and broad, like that of a bulldog.

It was inevitable, too, that the Thoroughbred should be crossed with the Quarter Horse to see what would come of the fusing of these two breeds. Janus, a grandson of the Godolphin Arabian, was chosen to sire a new line of Quarter Horses, and horsemen waited expectantly. Would the blood of Janus streamline the Quarter Horse? Would it create a new strain, a horse that could run an explosion race for an entire mile? No such thing happened. It was almost as if one Quarter Horse had been bred to another. The sons of Janus clung to their dams' character with bulldog tenacity. They were still blocky in build and faster than ever on the getaway.

But with each year, as more and more Thoroughbreds were imported, short racing died out. A weaker breed than the Quarter Horse would have vanished from the American scene, but he widened his territory. By river boat and by pack train he moved westward. And once again his brawn and his speed stood him in good stead. The cattlemen of the southwestern plains needed a chunky horse of immense power, one that could brace himself against the shock of a thousand pounds of wild steer at the end of a rope. They needed a horse that could pound over roughed-up land, swim rivers, push through brush, one that could maneuver a prize steer out of the herd or a runaway into the herd. In short, they needed the Quarter Horse. He took root in the southwest, especially in Texas, and as long as the range country endures, Texans say they will need him.

What of his racing career? Over and done with? It is just beginning again! Cattlemen, like the early settlers, need to work off the loneliness of their jobs. And so they get together and match the sprinting skill of their horses. Often they use any level stretch of land and have little private races with their neighbors. But sometimes they attend the big Quarter-Horse races, where the straightaways are smoothed and harrowed and there are grandstands and fence rails and all the fixings of fine tracks.

In 1947 a Quarter-Horse mare, Barbara B, raced against a famous Thoroughbred in a quarter-mile dash. The purpose was to prove the superiority of the Thoroughbred. But history only repeated itself. The Quarter Horse won!

Short racing has not changed much since colonial days. The track is nearly always a straightaway, and there is seldom a mechanical starting gate. The Quarter Horse jumps out from a standing position, and there is no crowding at the turns, for there are none. Each horse stays in his own lane or he is disqualified. At the start of the race the horses are often recalled again and again, and only an animal with a good disposition could keep up his eagerness to go.

Admirers of his placid disposition like to tell about the mare that pulled a washerwoman's cart down in Texas. The mare was a full sister to Kingfisher, a most C.A.Q.R.H. If she had wanted to, she could have flown through the streets, pitching clean shirts high into the air. Did she do it? No! She obeyed the traffic laws and stopped at each customer's house, nice as you please. As her brother became more famous, horsemen trailed the cart begging to buy or trade for the mare. But the washerwoman refused to sell. "I ain't a-going to do it," she flatly pronounced. "I raised up this filly foal on a bottle and she thinks I'm her mammy. If I lets her go, I'd only spend the cash and then where'd I be? Back scrubbing clothes again, and no horse to tote 'em."

For nearly three hundred years the Quarter Horse has been a distinct type but not until 1941 was he recognized with a stud book of his own. Now he is no longer just a type, no longer just a poor man's race horse. He has his own registry like other breeds. At last that bulldog tenacity has won! And, with little fox ears pricked, he goes on in the tradition of his forebears—race horse and cow pony both.

The Palomino

THE PALOMINO is not a breed but a color—the goldest color in the world. If you polished a gold coin all day long, still it would not take on the burnished brightness of a Palomino's coat.

When horsemen find a golden stallion that will always sire golden colts, like the goose that always laid a golden egg, then the Palomino will be a breed instead of a color. Meanwhile the tingle of excitement hovers over every ranch at foaling time, for only about half of the expected Palominos turn out to be true ones.

Outcroppings of golden horses appear among Tennessee Walkers, among American Saddle Horses, among Quarter Horses, but they are surprises, gold premium surprises. The names of these rare ones can be entered in their own registries, just as if they wore the sedate brown or bay coats of their ancestors. And, for good measure, they may be entered in the Palomino registry, too.

But it is different with the Palominos. The foal of a Palomino sire and dam may turn out not to be golden at all. He may be a white colorless creature with glassy pink or blue eyes. An outcast! When this happens, the stable owner turns away, heavy-hearted, wondering why in the world he ever wanted to raise golden horses.

But even in his disappointment he knows why. He is a gold prospector, hopeful of discovering a colt that will stamp his sons with pure gold.

The name Palomino is a delight to the imagination, but the meaning is not. It is Spanish and translated literally it means a pigeon or a stained shirt. Students of words insist that neither of these meanings could refer to the dazzling Palomino. They would like to change the name to Palomilla, the Spanish word for a flying moth or milk-white steed.

Horsemen agree that Palomilla may have a prettier thought behind it, but they would have you understand that a Palomino is *not* a white horse! His color is gold, and it can vary only in the degree of its goldness—three shades lighter or three shades darker than a newly minted coin. The only thing white about a Palomino is his mane and tail and white stockings, perhaps, or a blaze.

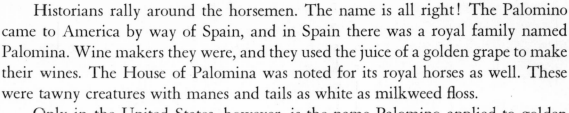

Historians rally around the horsemen. The name is all right! The Palomino came to America by way of Spain, and in Spain there was a royal family named Palomina. Wine makers they were, and they used the juice of a golden grape to make their wines. The House of Palomina was noted for its royal horses as well. These were tawny creatures with manes and tails as white as milkweed floss.

Only in the United States, however, is the name Palomino applied to golden horses. In Mexico they are Ysabellas, in honor of the Spanish queen, Isabella, and in Spain they are simply the Caballos de Oro, Horses of Gold. The clashing of swords over the name still goes on, but let a horseman hear you call a Palomino a Palomilla and he will walk off, wrinkling his nose in distaste.

A cattleman of Old California, Don Estaban, is credited with owning the first Palomino in America. In 1800, along about harvest time when range horses were brought in to thresh wheat, Don Estaban called his peons together. "To the one who finds the most beautiful horse in the country," he said, "I give much silver."

The peons, however, were unable to pick out any one horse, for in the roundup the herds were swallowed in dust and in the threshing they were all covered over with chaff. But a little Indian boy spied a glint of gold in the milling mob. He captured the golden colt, brushed him clean, washed his tail and mane, and presented him to Don Estaban. This one, the story goes, was the first true Palomino found in the New World, and he sired many golden colts.

Mexicans tell a different story altogether. One starless night, they say, two Indians stole into the hacienda of a Spanish grandee and spirited away a pure-white stallion and a buckskin mare. A year later the mare escaped from the Indians and fled back home with a little blonde filly at her heels.

The stories are alike in one respect. Both golden creatures were remarkable for more than their color. They had the refined, shapely heads, the underlying dark skin, and the dark eyes of the Arabian. Today these are the marks of distinction in the Palomino. One registry will not accept a Palomino unless his skin is dark beneath the gold and his eyes hazel or brown.

Palominos flourished in numbers for a while, and then they began to peter out because they lost their Arabian look. Who wanted to be seen riding a jug-headed scrubby creature, even if his color did vie with the sun? The other established breeds could furnish better riding horses, and color was only skin deep after all.

But was it? California, always partial to its gold, began to "breed up" the Palominos. Horsemen brought in chestnut and bay Arabians, Thoroughbreds, American Saddle Horses, and Quarter Horses and bred them to their Palominos. They wanted to produce more than color, and they did! They developed three fixed types of Palominos—the stock horse, the pleasure horse, and the parade horse.

The Palomino stock horses are really glorified Quarter Horses, and Roy Rogers' Trigger is the most famous of them all. They can do what any good Quarter Horse can do. They can help brand steers with the best of them and race the short distances to win. One golden stock horse could even take a lasso in his teeth and rope a little dogie alone. And the Palomino, Gold King Bailey, in race after race with Quarter Horses and Thoroughbreds finished away out in front. He won so often they nicknamed him Galloping Gold.

The pleasure Palominos often have American Saddle Horse blood in their veins and they high-step the bridle paths, weaving in and out the dappled shade like golden shuttles in the sun.

But it is the parade Palomino that is best known. In the Tournament of Roses in Pasadena the Palominos are, for many, more stirring than the millions of flowers that make up the floats. It is the Palominos that draw shrieks of joy from the children, especially when Leo Carillo's Conquistadore dances the fandango or when the sheriff's entire posse of golden horses marches by to the *oom-pah, oom-pah* of the high-school bands.

Life for a parade Palomino is a round of music and excitement. He could enter a parade unadorned, but instead his saddle and bridle gleam with silver until the horse's coat and his trappings outshine each other. He seems to sense that his business is show business and the heavy silver saddles are his costume.

At Fiesta time in Santa Barbara, Palominos are actors in a play. They carry swashbuckling *caballeros* down from the hills into the full light of a stage, where they dance a quadrille. But not even the measured beauty of their steps equals the moment when the audience first spies them on the hilltop with the moon striking full upon their golden coats and the deep velvet sky for a backdrop.

Palominos are at their golden best in pageants, parades, and fiestas, and they have become so popular that horsemen from all over the country are going west to find them. A new gold rush is on! Men seek Palomino gold.

The
Shetland Pony

THE STORY of the Shetland pony is a Cinderella story. Sheltie, as he is called in Great Britain, started out in life as a drudge. In the bleak and stormy Shetland Islands north of Scotland he was a miniature draft animal, a chunk. He looked like a drafter, with his blocky build, and he worked like one, patiently and all day long.

It was Sheltie who carried bulging baskets of peat down from the hills to heat the little cottages in the glens. It was Sheltie who carried sacks of seaweed up from the shore to fertilize the tiny farm patches. And it was Sheltie who worked in front of a small wooden plow while his thrifty master spread seaweed in the furrows.

Never was there another pony who filled so many needs. For long years he furnished the only transportation on the islands. Even though he stood but thirty-nine inches high, the people rode him wherever they went. If the cluster of shops that made up a "toon" was twenty miles away, or even thirty, they often rode him there without stopping! Sometimes the rider was a man, hard-muscled and big. Sometimes it was a plump woman whose skirt billowed out like a feather bed, and all that showed of poor Sheltie was his pert little head and his grand sweeping tail.

But Sheltie bore his burdens as patiently as he bore the weather. Drizzle, drizzle, drizzle. Wind, wind, wind. What did it matter? His wild mop of a mane made a shield for his eyes, and his long shaggy hair made a good raincoat. Rain-and windproof, he faced the brawling blast of the gales and the spindrift of the sea.

Sheltie worked as a pit pony, too, in the mines of England. Here he pulled coal cars through the long cramped passageways, his lungs breathing coal dust and hot stuffy air, his ears deafened by the tumbling lumps of spilling coal. Some of the pit ponies never, in all their lives, came up for a breath of clean, fresh air. And they could never rear up in play without butting their heads against the low roofs. In fact, a pit pony forgot how to play. He just worked the days around and slept the nights around, and lived and died in the pits.

But at last a happy day arrived. The mines were electrified, and there was no

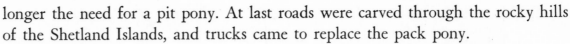

longer the need for a pit pony. At last roads were carved through the rocky hills of the Shetland Islands, and trucks came to replace the pack pony.

Now a happy thought came to the islanders. Why could not their husky little drafters become children's ponies the world over? For answer, they hoisted the squealing creatures aboard steamers by means of slings and cranes, and off the ponies sailed—far across the sea to America.

At the end of the journey a curious thing happened. All in a twinkling life for Sheltie was transformed. It was as if some magic wand had touched him. The wand had five pudgy fingers that tippeted lightly over his shaggy coat, then wriggled deep into the thick warm fur beneath. Wide, ecstatic eyes looked long into his own. Small palms reached out to cup his muzzle. And suddenly in the touching it seemed that two long-lost creatures were restored to each other.

Children everywhere claimed the tiny pony for their own, and Sheltie basked in happiness. From a workaday drudge he became a fun-loving playmate. No door was closed to him, for he taught himself how to slide bolts, open gates, rattle latches. His long lips became expert in plucking caps from children's heads or handkerchiefs from pockets. And always these little tricks ended in a rousing game of tag.

As for work, there was none! A canter over the countryside with a lightweight child on his back was no work. Or pulling a basketcart of children to a picnic. He *liked* picnics. To him they meant cool streams with forget-me-nots growing in tasty clumps along the banks, and a tossed apple core to munch for dessert.

As a child's playmate Sheltie no longer needed to look like a chunk. In fact, a child could ride more securely if he were able to clasp the pony with his knees. With that in mind breeders began to develop the American type Shetland, slimmer of barrel but no taller.

And so with the years there came to be two types of Shetlands—the slender American and the English draft. While the English type is usually solid black, brown, or bay, the American is often piebald. Children seem just as eager to adopt one as the other.

Parents, too, are completely won by the Shetland's gentle charm. And they have found that the way to keep him gentle is to make certain he is neither overfed nor mistreated.

To understand the care and keeping of our present-day Shetlands, we need to peer into their past with pony-like curiosity. Picture those lonely Shetland Islands—so lonely that when the Romans discovered them they named the group Ultima Thule, or the edge of the world. Picture the wind, lashing and pounding the land so that trees grew dwarfed or not at all. And picture the rocks whipped bare of soil except for a thin layer in the glens. The people had to work so hard to wrest a living that they needed a sturdy little beast to work with them. It was the Sheltie that became their farmhand. But in return for his labors there was little the people could give. All they could do after the day's work was to throw him a bit of hay or turn him out to the coarse grass. And if the spring was slow in coming, there was often no fodder at all except heather or prickly seaweed left by the tide. But one thing the Shetlanders did give their ponies in abundance, and that was comradeship. Their low graystone cottages had but one door, and when the wind lashed into a fury and the sea battered at the rocks and went up in funnels of spume, then man and pony hurried through the same door and found warmth and comfort around the glowing peat fire.

It needs only a little imagining to see that our Shelties, too, will thrive on the same treatment—the simplest of fare, the daily canter, and the open door to our hearts.

The Welsh Mountain Pony

BLUE RIBBONS, red ribbons, yellow ribbons, white ribbons! In show classes for ponies, sometimes there is more than one kind of champion— the blue-ribbon pony and also the boy whose pony just misses.

For one hurt second the boy blinks back his tears, pretending he doesn't care. And then in a flash he really doesn't. He remembers the time his pony carried him down the slippery sides of a stone quarry until they stood in the very bottom of the cup, then up and up again to the dizzying rim above the whole wide world. And he remembers the day his pony jumped across a deep ravine and all the others balked.

Remembering all this, he strokes the sleek neck, swings astride, and bravely trots his pony out of the ring behind the winner.

The judge, with a deep sigh of relief, mops his forehead. "There go *two* champions," he mutters to no one at all, "the light gray Welsh and that thorough-bred boy astride the dark one!"

More and more, big shows and small ones are offering classes for the best ponies, and more and more the finely made Welsh is coming out of obscurity to carry away the blue ribbons. He is frequently the graduation mount for the boy or girl whose legs have grown too long for the Shetland.

Who would suspect that the ancestors of this delicately made pony were half-wild refugees, hiding in the craggy mountains of Wales, escaping one enemy only to meet another?

First they were hunted and tracked down by the sheep herders, who looked upon them as thieves of the juicy grasses belonging to their sheep. Often the herders would capture a band, kill off the colts for food, and throw the scraps to their dogs. These sheep dogs were strong as wolves and, once having tasted pony meat, they hunted the little fellows themselves, stealing up on them silently without the least warning. A mare would be grazing peacefully and suddenly she would look up to see a snarling dog ready to leap at her foal. In a flash she was between them, springing at the killer with her forefeet, then driving her young one into

a gallop through narrow passes, up a steep scarp, leaping from ledge to ledge until at last they were safe in the folds of the mountains. Tiny colts only a few weeks old had to learn to take their first jumps to save their lives. Some were strong enough to escape; when they did they became nimble and wondrously wise.

But the sheep herders and their dogs were only small annoyances. The law was a bigger enemy. It reached out from the throne of England and shoved the ponies deeper and deeper into the mountains. King Henry VIII, with a gesture of his jeweled hands, decreed that "little horses and nags of small stature must be eliminated from the common grazing grounds." As a result many ponies were killed and others fled into the mountain fastnesses. Here they found a quiet tableland high above the grazing grounds, and although the rocky soil furnished scanty herbage, the air was clean and clear, and sparkling cold drinking water bubbled down the mountainsides.

Yet even here they were attacked. Now winter was their enemy, biting with the sharp fangs of wind, howling into their ears, spitting hail and sleet at them. Sometimes the herds had to sneak down into the valleys to find food.

But hardships strengthen. And so it was with the ponies. Those that survived developed hoofs as flinty as the rocks they climbed, and hocks and haunches like steel springs, and lung and heart room to send them traveling like will-o'-the-wisps.

No! Enemies did not stamp out the spirited Welsh pony. They only made him stronger, hardier, wiser; and, above all, they preserved the purity of his blood. By not mixing with other breeds he has remained distinct.

There is a fineness about the Welsh pony, a kind of nobility in his bearing as if he knows that in his veins flows the blood of the Arabian. It shows in the refinement of his head, in his dished face, his "pint pot" muzzle, even in his color. Never is there a piebald or a skewbald among the true Welsh mountain ponies. They are bay, brown, or chestnut, with grays predominating, just as in the Arab.

At first people wondered how the blood of the horse of the desert found its way into the Welsh mountains. Then as they began to ask questions, it became clear. In faraway times had not the Romans invaded Wales? And was it not likely they had brought with them the spoils of their campaigns in Africa—the desert ponies that satisfied their eye for beauty and their need for quick flight? For four hundred years the Romans had occupied Wales, importing more and more Arabian horses which mingled with the native wild herds. Their offspring became pack ponies for the Romans, but they did not look like pack ponies at all. They had the elegant form of the Arabian, and they were fleet of foot like the Arabian—in truth, they were diminutive Arabians.

But Henry VIII was not one to appreciate the fine symmetry of these ponies. Hence his decree which almost wiped out the Welsh Mountain Pony.

It is a long road, however, that has no turning. Today the ponies still live high up on the tablelands, but when winter overstays, they are not afraid to nimble-foot down the mountains. The hand of man is friendly now. Even when it captures some of the fillies and colts for breeding purposes. The curious truth is that these creatures thrive in captivity; yet, no matter where they go, they cling to their wild pony characteristics. They jump a brush hurdle as high and clean as if a sheep dog were snapping at their heels, and at the walk or trot they pick up their feet and place them carefully as though testing the earth for loose pieces of shale. Even in America they have this "heather step."

Perhaps the ponies of Wales are like the Welsh people who, in a changing world, cling steadfastly to their ancient language and customs. They are like them in another respect, too. On the Welsh coat of arms a motto describes the people. The words of the motto are *Ich Dien,* "I serve." Every Welshman who understands pony character insists that *Ich Dien* describes the mountain pony, too, for he serves his master well.

No wonder he is a champion! And when the blue ribbon comes his way, he wears it in his headstall as if to the manner born.

The Chincoteague Pony

Five miles out in the Atlantic Ocean, off the eastern shore of Virginia, lie two tiny wind-rippled islands. They are as rich in horse lore as a mince pie is rich in raisins. Chincoteague (pronounced *Shin-ko-teeg*) is the smaller island, seven miles long and just twenty-one inches above the sea. Assateague is the bold outrider, protecting little Chincoteague from high winds and high seas.

Oystermen, clam diggers, and boat builders live on Chincoteague, but the outer island is left to the wild things, the wild ponies and the birds.

How the ponies came there is legend, but Grandpa Beebe, one of the natives, says, "Legends be the only stories as is true; facts are fine, far as they go, but they're water bugs skittering atop the water. Legends, now, they go deep down and bring up the heart of a story."

And so legend says that, way back in the yesterdays, a Spanish galleon was bowling along the deep when a great storm came up and blew the ship off its course. In her hold she carried live cargo—Spanish moor ponies headed for the mines of Peru. The ponies smelled the storm and plunged against their rough-built stalls, trying to escape. But it was the sea that finally set them free. It drove the ship onto a reef, cracking her hull open and spewing the ponies out of their dark prisons. In spite of the waves and the wreckage they thrashed their way to the nearest shore, and the first land they touched was the beach of Assateague.

Not a solitary soul lived on the whole island. And there were no fences anywhere. Only wide stretches of sand, and marshland with salt-flavored grass, and piney woods. Land and sea and sky were theirs, to be shared only with the black skimmer birds and the blue herons and clacking geese.

Always before, the ponies had been accustomed to man's care. Now they had to rustle their own living. In winter they huddled in the woods, stripping the bark of pine trees, eating bark and needles, too, and they ate the myrtle leaves that stayed green. For drinking water they broke little mirrors of ice with their hoofs and drank the brackish water beneath. And they grew rough winter coats which took the place of man-made shelter. Snow sometimes sifted onto their backs and made a white

fleece without melting, so heavy were their coats. Who minded winter? Not the ponies.

The Gingoteague Indians who used to hunt on the island now stayed far away. From their canoes they could see the ponies running wild along the shore, and the sight filled them with a nameless fear.

The white men, however, were unafraid. A few poled over to Assateague and built houses there, but by that time the ponies had grown to such numbers that they overran the island, trampling cleared plots and eating corn blades as fast as they pushed through the ground. In dismay the people gathered their belongings and sculled back across the channel to live on Chincoteague.

Today the outer island of Assateague is still a wildlife refuge, except for Pony Penning Day. On that day, late in July, the watermen on Chincoteague turn cowboy. Still wearing their fishermen's caps and boots, they ferry their own riding horses over to Assateague to round up the wild ponies. It is the oldest roundup in America! Through bog and brier and bullrushes they ride, spooking the ponies out of little hidden places, driving them down to Tom's Cove. At exactly low tide a signal is given and the wild herds, colts and all, are driven into the sea for the swim across to Chincoteague. The channel boils with ponies—stallions neighing to their mares, mares whinnying to their colts, colts squealing in panic. And all across the channel, oyster boats ride herd on the ponies, keeping them swimming toward Chincoteague.

At last, wet and blown, the wild things scramble out of the water, and a cheer goes up from the throng of visitors who have come to see the biggest Wild West Show of the east. In their mind's eye they are selecting their own colt to buy at tomorrow's sale, for Chincoteague ponies, captured early, make good, friendly mounts. The mares and stallions, of course, are too wild. After a day of being penned up in big corrals, they are driven back again to Assateague for another year of freedom.

Why are some of the ponies big and some small? Some solid color and some daubed with white? The reason is that at one time a Shetland stallion was turned loose on Assateague to run with the wild ponies. His influence is seen in the smallness of stature and the two-toned coloring of many.

The pony, Misty of Chincoteague, is one of these, and she is strangely marked. Over her withers there is a white spot spread out like a map of the United States, and on her side there is a marking in the shape of a plow.

As a foal she seemed more mist than real. Her coat was a soft fusion of silver and gold, and her eyelashes were gold and wonderfully long. In contrast to her shaggy sire and dam she appeared like something from a cloud. During the sale no one dared touch her, for her wild sire glowered at people through the ambush of his forelock. And as Misty lay sleeping, her mother made fenceposts of her legs, keeping her foal safe inside them.

But after Misty's sire was driven back to Assateague, Grandpa Beebe and his two grandchildren kept Misty for a very special purpose. She was to be the heroine of a book! They cared for her and gentled her and, true to their promise, when fall came they crated Misty and shipped her to her new owner. On a chilly rain-soaked night she arrived at her destination near Chicago, and when the crate was opened, there stood a miserable little object. Head down, tail tucked in, eyes and nose running, and so stiff-legged that even with the crate opened she only stood, snuffling and cold and afraid.

The author was torn by conflicting emotions. Where was the map on Misty's withers? Where was the plow on her side? There were no markings at all! From head to tail she was the color of sooty snow, and woolly as a bear. That Grandpa Beebe! Had he shipped the wrong pony? And suddenly the author did not care. Here was a creature that needed help—a hot mash to eat and a warm bed and companionship. And so the little book character and her storyteller spent that stormy night in the stall together, and the little thing slept with her head cradled in human hands.

Winter passed. Spring came, and Misty rolled and rolled in the grass until her winter coat came off in great swatches for the birds to carry away. And, wonder of wonders, there was the gold coat; and there were the white markings, one in the shape of a map and the other a plow. Grandpa Beebe *had* sent the right pony after all!

Misty is now a grown-up mare, but her coat still changes with the seasons. She has forgotten her wild ancestors and has adopted people completely. She actually seems to be one of them, traveling as gaily as a person, acting on television, attending a meeting with librarians, going up in elevators with them, visiting a suite in one of the fine hotels. She even refreshed herself in the wash basin, lipping the pure water so different from the brackish pools of Assateague. The librarians asked: "Can this be the same creature whose ancestors ran wild and free?"

The question caused a wondering. Was Misty unhappy? Did she long for her freedom? But, back home again, the storyteller had only to look out of her window to see Misty running to the fence to meet a group of children. As she shook hands with each one, it was plain that Misty had found her own kind of happiness—with people.

No one has ever told her she is not one of them. She wouldn't believe it anyway.

The Burro or Donkey

LIKE THE HUGE EARS of the burro, history casts long, long shadows. When gold seekers rushed to California more than a century ago, they needed a sure-footed little animal as much as they needed their picks and pans. They went prospecting deep into gulches and up and down mountainsides to find precious particles of gold. The trails were steep and tortuous, and only a burro could keep his footing and balance a topheavy load besides. At night, free of saddle and pack, the small mouse-colored beast would stand naked and alone, snuffing the wind, trying to gather in the scent of green things. Then, braying as if laughing at his foolish hopes, he would lower his white muzzle to munch the scrawny shrub at his feet.

The prospector, too, chewed his sour-dough biscuits while visions of plump turkeys danced in his head. Supper over and the campfire in embers, the grizzled old master would talk to his silent partner. Dreams of great wealth were poured into the long ears, which swung back and forth like semaphores wagging sympathy.

Today, a whole century later, the self-same comradeship between burro and prospector goes on. Today's prospector, however, seeks uranium, not gold. And instead of packing a panning tray, he wears a Geiger counter slung over his shoulder. Like some doctor with his stethoscope he goes along listening to the crust of the earth. Instead of heartbeats he listens for a rapid burst of short sharp clicks which may mean the presence of uranium. Once again the burro has found his place in the sun, carrying the most incredible loads for his master—cooking utensils and blankets and boxes, and sometimes a pet rooster for an alarm clock. "He needs no winding," the prospector says. "Never has to be set for four o'clock, and always crows off on time."

It takes a million pounds of ore to produce a thimbleful of uranium, and the distance traveled to discover a rich vein is often long and discouraging. Today, too, the burro is not only pack animal; he is also confidant and friend.

Ever since Bible times the patient plodding burro has been man's wistful companion. He carried on his small back Abraham, the patriarch, who journeyed

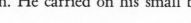

from place to place as a wandering pilgrim. And he carried Jacob six hundred miles into Mesopotamia. And he pulled plows for the children of Israel, and he carried packs so enormous that, as the Bible says, he crouched down between his two burdens.

In the Old World he was known as the ass, but when the Spaniards introduced him into the New World, they used the Spanish name, *burro*. The change in name, however, did not change his status. Hour for hour he did more work than any other animal, four-legged or two. He transported live, flapping fish from the seacoast to Mexico City, where the pompous rulers waited impatiently for their dinners. And he carried great cargoes of gold and silver from the mines to the seaports. His life was all work, with only short recesses for nibbling the bitter leaves of the mesquite bush.

But in spite of it all he never appeared gaunt or downtrodden, and his fame as a sure-footed fellow traveled down the centuries. Today, there are well over a million burros going about their business in Mexico as if planes and trains and jeeps and tractors didn't exist. They carry charcoal down from the hills and freight to the railroads, and when their work is done, they carry their masters to little straw-hut villages.

There is much talk about the burro's stupidity, but he's a smart one at hide-and-seek. He plants himself quietly in the shade of a dusty bush, knowing he and the bush are all of one color. So still he stands that his irate master often passes right by. Who, then, is the stupid one? When the game has gone on long enough, the burro often ends it with a great raucous heehaw.

The heart of a burro, they say, is expressed in his ecstatic braying. There is no other sound quite like it. The beast seems to be wrenching his soul to produce it. He raises his head to the heavens, throws wide his jaws, swells out his nostrils, and then begins such a wheezing and rasping and snuffling as if forty steam whistles were trying to escape into two little syllables, a hee and a haw. And all the while, he closes his dreamy, doelike eyes as if this were the supreme moment of his life. Because of his "melodic" voice he is humorously called the mountain canary and his fillies and foals are called chicks.

One little mountain canary had a bray as welcome as bird song in spring. He wintered in the warm Grand Canyon near Bright Angel Creek, where he became known as Brighty. Along toward flytime he would lope up the creek to a cool plateau and let himself be captured. Usually he appeared at one of the summer camps and went to work as water boy, carrying spring water down from the mountains. Between trips he would let children ride on his back, but he seemed allergic to grownups, always tossing them skyward. He was such a good worker, however, that the campers hung a bell on his neck to keep track of him and they tied him at night. But when, in fall, Brighty decided to go home, he gnawed his rope in two. Then he walked away with just the right swaying motion to keep the little clapper in the bell from tinkling. Once out of hearing, he scampered down the slopes to his winter resort in the chasm. Nobody was going to tell Brighty when to work, and no one ever did.

Maybe Brighty was a throwback to his ancestor, the wild ass, who ran free in Africa long, long ago. This wild ancestor, however, was more fierce than Brighty. He fought with hoof and tooth, protecting his young against lions and leopards. He fought, too, to be monarch of his herd. Each stallion, or jack, headed a harem of mares, or jennies who, with their colts, made up a big family of thirty or more. The jack herded his family from one lush grazing ground to another, guarding the members jealously from leaders of other bands. But once domesticated the jack lost his fiery ways and became the patient plodding creature he is today.

As the "poor relation" of the horse, the burro knows no currycomb and no brush. His coarse coat grows as it pleases, and the wisp of his tail looks more and more like a worn-out hearth broom with each mile of travel. His mane is scrubby and erect like a crew haircut. Altogether he is a creature that needs no grooming nor does he want any. Trees make fine scratching posts, and for him baths in hot shimmering sand are good and cleansing.

While tractors have often taken the place of horses, no machine has been found to equal the burro as the beast of burden of the Southwest. He has replaced the Indian runners, but no man nor man-made thing has ever replaced him.

In our great city squares one never sees a marble statue, or even a bronze one, dedicated to the burro; yet honor and glory have not passed him by. People of humble ways have chosen him! The Mexican peon feels a kinship for his *burritito,* as he affectionately calls him, because they are both meek and lowly servitors.

And the man, Jesus, rejected the horse and chose the little long-eared beast to carry him into Jerusalem on that first Palm Sunday. A very great multitude, the Scriptures say, spread their garments in the way and strewed the path with palm branches, but the sure-footed little beast picked his way through and over them and entered triumphantly into the city.

There are those who say Jesus rewarded his patient burden-bearer with an emblem. Ever since, from mane to tail, he has worn a dark stripe, and at the withers a horizontal one—for all the world like the symbol of the cross.

The Mule

WHEN APRIL COMES IN, down in Columbia, Tennessee, the people feel like saying thank you to the mule for all he has done for them. And so they invite mules from far and wide—the little cotton mules, the large farm mules, the still larger sugar mules, and the mammoth draft mules—to a big parade and celebration in their honor.

Of course, the owners are invited, too, and for weeks ahead of time they get ready. They begin giving their mules a daily grooming so their coats will shine, and they get out the old surrey and wash the fringe on top, and they polish harness until it winks in the sun.

Meanwhile a committee of judges scours the countryside for just the right mule to represent all mules, to be King-for-a-Day. He must have large feet, a strong back, and abundant muscle. And of course his coat should be nice and sleek, and his ears long, wonderfully long, with a pert little knob at each tip. Must he be free of blemish or flaw? No, if the hair of his neck and mane is worn by the harness, the judges like him even better. In muledom proof of work is a badge of honor.

While one committee seeks a fine mule to be King, another combs the county for a pretty girl to crown him. And still a third committee is checking on the crown, seeing that none of the rhinestone jewels is missing.

First Monday of April comes. It is the biggest "mulesta" in American history. No work today! Down out of the hills and up from the valleys come hundreds of mules, in clown costumes, in flower costumes, in no costumes at all. They march in singles, they march in spans, they march in fours and sixes. Some are ridden by boys and girls, some are driven to old-timey gigs, and the little mule colts are shown in hand.

As for the King Mule, he rides in an elegant mule-drawn float, and he looks as pleased as a child on a merry-go-round. His eyes and ears are taking in the swirls of pink cotton candy, the flags waving, the rollicking music, and the shower of serpentine. When his float reaches the courthouse, the entire procession comes to a halt while the pretty girl places the jeweled crown between his ears.

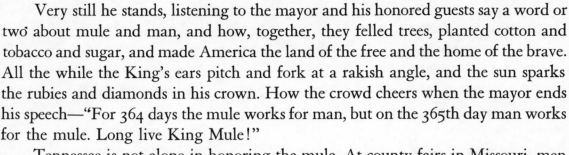

Very still he stands, listening to the mayor and his honored guests say a word or two about mule and man, and how, together, they felled trees, planted cotton and tobacco and sugar, and made America the land of the free and the home of the brave. All the while the King's ears pitch and fork at a rakish angle, and the sun sparks the rubies and diamonds in his crown. How the crowd cheers when the mayor ends his speech—"For 364 days the mule works for man, but on the 365th day man works for the mule. Long live King Mule!"

Tennessee is not alone in honoring the mule. At county fairs in Missouri, men with rulers go around measuring the "wingspread" of the show mules' ears. One mule named Double Elastic held the record for some time. Her stretch was thirty-two inches from tip to tip.

Whence came the long-eared mule? Who is his sire and who his dam? He is a strange mixture, neither horse nor donkey but a combination of both. His mother is a horse mare and his father a donkey, and he inherits admirable qualities from each. From his mother he gets courage, speed, strength; and from his father, patience and sure-footedness and the ability to grow sleek on nothing but grass. He has his father's head, too—the white nose, the donkey ears—and his lusty bray as well.

But his mule-mindedness, ah, this is strictly his own. Some men call it stubbornness; muleteers call it wisdom. They say the mule knows three times as much as the horse, and they count the ways. If his load is too heavy, he waits for you to lighten it. If he has put in enough hours for one day, he stages a strike. If the water in a creek is unfit to drink, he won't touch a drop. If the weather is unbearably hot, he slows his pace, and no amount of prodding will hurry him. If his pasture is hilly, he eats uphill instead of down so he won't have so far to bend! If he is climbing a steep hill, he stops midway of his own accord to take a breather; he doesn't wait for man to whoa him.

Horses, on the other hand, have been known to work themselves into exhaustion. And if they run away, they sometimes dash blindly against a fence or plunge over a cliff. But the mule practices safety and moderation in all things. He never overeats, never drinks icy water when he himself is steaming, and if things don't suit him, he doesn't snuffle and whinner, he just goes to sleep as if it were not worth bothering about.

The climax of his day comes at sundown when he gets out of his collar and harness. Then, with great delight, he rolls and rolls and heehaws until his master feels like doing the same thing.

It was George Washington who made the mule popular in America. After the Revolutionary War he put his mind to the business of peace—to scientific farming. He had heard of the enormous Catalonian donkeys in Spain and of the fine work mules they sired. He wanted to introduce them into America because, as he put it, "their cheap keeping is much in their favor." But the Spanish government had a law against exporting their jacks. When the King of Spain, however, heard that the General himself was interested, he felt that his country had been honored and he issued a royal order to send two of the finest jacks in the kingdom as a gift. One of them died aboard ship, but the other arrived at Mount Vernon in fine fettle and, on a summer morning, there he stood, right on the piazza of the mansion house!

General Washington was mightily impressed. "From him," he said to the little gathering that had assembled, "I hope to secure a race of extraordinary goodness which will stock the country. He is indeed a Royal Gift, and henceforward that shall be his name."

Within the next few years the President mated several of his mares to Royal Gift and got some strapping mules. They were so tough that he put them to work at an early age. Friends and neighbors shook their heads in amazement. How fat and sleek the mule kept in spite of his work! How he pulled and plowed and cultivated on the hottest days! They wanted mules, too. And so, before very long, the whole Virginia countryside was dotted with the long-eared sons and daughters of Royal Gift.

George Washington would be astounded and pleased if he could know that today the mule is more valuable than the horse; that is, his average price is higher. Isn't this an incredible fact when one remembers that some race horses sell for tens of thousands of dollars? Another fact that might have caused the President to chuckle, and the King of Spain, too, is that American jacks have since been exported to Spain to improve their breed!

When mules die, they leave no children. None at all. The only purpose for which they are bred is work. And they don't seem to object at all. In fact, even in Tennessee when the excitement and flag waving of Mule Day are over, the King Mule himself seems glad to be rid of his crown and to get on with his spring plowing.

Men of the South consider the mule indispensable. He seems part of their life, part of their landscape. And, when April comes in, a mule's ears against the sky are as grand and glorious a sight as the dogwood and redbud in bloom!

The Routine
of Happiness

A HORSE'S ACTIONS are based on habit. Variety may be the very spice of life for people, but for horses routine is their peculiar happiness. Eat. Sleep. Work. At the same time every day. Year in, year out. Time without end.

There was once a work horse that lived exactly by the clock. His name was Charley and he furnished the power that operated the presses for a printing house. Every morning, just as the factory whistle blew, Charley was hooked to a pole connected to a shaft. And before the blast had pinched off in silence, Charley was at work, walking around in a circle, turning the shaft which had a big wheel at the top of it. By means of a pulley the big wheel was connected to a smaller wheel, and as Charley turned the shaft, the pulleys inside the factory went around and around and worked the printing presses.

All morning and all afternoon, too, Charley walked in this perpetual circle, hearing nothing but the flump of his footsteps and the hum of the presses; seeing nothing but his path and the sparrows that bathed in the dust he made.

Charley liked the sameness of his days. They were not drear to him at all. He knew what to expect and when. He could have kicked over the traces and run away to green fields, but such a thought never occurred to him. And Mr. Dooley, the happy Irishman who took care of him, knew he could be trusted. After starting Charley off, Mr. Dooley went about his own business and did not show up again until noontime, when he came striding along with a nosebag of rustling oats.

Afternoons were just like the mornings. Walk around and around. Turn the shaft. Swish flies. Sweat and dry off. Keep walking. Walk the sun out of sight.

When the evening whistle blew, Charley stopped as if a stone wall had suddenly risen before him. This was a pleasant time of day—Mr. Dooley unhooking him and making little confidential remarks, and men and boys whistling down the stairs and out of the building. One always stopped to give Charley a slice of apple. The fragrant juices tickled his senses; he could smell the apple long before he saw it. Then *crunch, crunch,* and the sweet juice slaking his thirst. Life was good. It had a pleasant pattern.

106

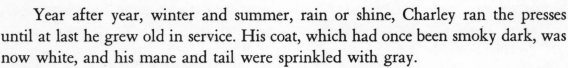

Year after year, winter and summer, rain or shine, Charley ran the presses until at last he grew old in service. His coat, which had once been smoky dark, was now white, and his mane and tail were sprinkled with gray.

One spring morning Charley's orderly world suddenly went topsy-turvy. A shining black horse was brought into his stable and cross-tied almost in front of his stall. And Mr. Dooley was putting Charley's collar over the young black's neck and Charley's bit into the young one's mouth!

Instinctively Charley disliked the newcomer. He broke into a snort and pinned his ears back. Mr. Dooley went right on with his buckling. "By the hole in the seat of me pants," he laughed, "I do believe the old crayture's jealous already!"

Then the young horse was backed between the shafts of a wagon and led out into the morning. And, before Charley knew what was happening, *he* was being tied to the tailboard. He tugged at his halter, trying to turn toward his familiar circle, but the wagon was starting up and he was being pulled out onto a hard dirt road. Past his factory. Past other factories. Past houses. Across a railroad track. And always he could hear the hoofbeats ahead.

Strange, new smells began mingling in his nostrils—plowed earth and apple blossoms. Suddenly the hoofbeats ahead came to a stop, and Mr. Dooley was at his side, untying him, now leading him through an open gate into a green pasture. Then one by one his shoes were pulled off and even his halter was taken away.

" 'Tis little I can think to say, Charley," Mr. Dooley murmured. "Ye see, it's like this way, Charley; ye've earned a rest. The grass and trees is buddin', and it's a sootherin' piece o' sod ye got here. Ain't it, Charley? Aye. And I'll come back every once and again to give ye a whiskin' over and an apple out of me own wages, and may the Lord preserve ye, Charley."

Without a backward look Mr. Dooley gathered up the horseshoes, put the halter over his arm, and went out the gate. He clucked to the young horse, and the wagon went creaking on its way.

Charley began to tremble violently. He threw back his head and sent out a great cry of loneliness. He ran along the fence line ahead of the black horse, whinnying him to stop, imploring him. But the young horse did not hesitate. He trotted briskly along, step by step, until the sound of his hoofs and the creaking of the wheels grew fainter and fainter and then died away.

For a long time Charley stood in the corner as if he were picketed to the earth. He had a kind of naked feeling without his shoes and his harness, and he felt a nothingness inside. There was no one in sight but an old hound dog, sniffing along a hedgerow, bent on bird business. Slowly Charley footed his way toward the dog and, as he walked, he felt a wet coolness under his feet. He pawed the grass, stirring up a delicate scent. He tore a mouthful and found it tender and succulent. He forgot about the dog and fell to grazing; and he grazed the morning away.

Toward noon the bright sun beat down on his back and a stupor came over him. He sought the shade of a big cottonwood tree and there, with a sweet quid of grass in his mouth, he slept standing, dozing the afternoon away.

For a few days he enjoyed his barefoot freedom. Then, gradually, a great longing filled him. He missed his old way of life. Morning came and no one said, "Move over with ye, Charley. Och! But it's a grand smiling day!"

And there was no familiar path to tread, and no nosebag at noon or apple at night. Only earth and sky, and between them an aching emptiness. The grass seemed to lose its flavor, and Charley ate less and less of it. He grew gaunt and his underlip hung loose, quivering like that of an old man who cries easily. Mr. Dooley came to visit him and shook his head. "We got the poor crayture here just in time all right," he said to no one at all. "His work days is done for sure."

And then one early morning the wind blew across the town, picking up smells and sounds on its way. The whistle of Charley's old factory came to him faintly.

The sound pulled a trigger in his mind and fired him to act. Resolutely he headed for the cottonwood tree and began walking around it, buckling down to his work as if he were pulling the pole that turned the shaft. Around and around he went. Trudge and turn. Keep walking. Swish flies. Sweat and dry off. Trample the grass. Bend it down. Wear it down. Wear the path bare. Keep going!

All morning he traveled the circle. At noon the faraway whistle stopped him. He left his tree and grazed his way toward the creek. There he rolled in the mud along its banks, first this way, then that. Afterward he stretched out in the sun and snoozed a bit until the afternoon whistle woke him.

Again the trigger in his mind! Struggling to his feet, he went back to his self-appointed work. All afternoon he wore the path deeper. By evening the wind had turned about and Charley could not hear the whistle, but his time sense told him when to stop. He quit work suddenly and began frisking around the pasture like a youngster let out of school. He waded in the creek and drank deep; then he plashed until the water spattered all over his belly. He felt good!

Now Charley knew what to do each day, and the hours ran together as smoothly as water flowing downhill. In time a great change came over him. He didn't look like a colt exactly, nor did his gray hair turn black. But his happiness showed in so many ways—in the luster in his eye, in the spring of his step, in the round-barreled look of him! Growing old was not bad at all, so long as there was something to do. Charley had made his own work, and he was back in harness again—the good, comfortable harness of routine.

No Sugar, Thank You!

THE LITTLE COLT sniffed, and the smell of morning tickled in his nose and the whirly wind stirred the whiskers in his ears. He tossed his head, snorting and squealing. It was good—morning and the wind and having his mother this close.

He kicked up to the sky and down to the earth, and with a wee flirt of his tail scampered across the meadow. In long easy strides his mother overtook him and now she is alongside, pacing him, keeping him steady on the trot, schooling him.

Big hoofs and little hoofs go winging along the grass, making fresh tracks· in the dew. Only the fence line can stop them, and the mare slows, bunting her young one away from it. They stand for a moment to blow and to snort, but the wind teases them on again. They wheel and are off, galloping now, drinking the bracy air deep into their lungs, drinking up the morning.

Schooling—how easy it is! Trotting. Galloping. Using your tail as a rudder, kinking it around the curves. "You, young'un, keep away from that fence! Keep away or I'll bunt you away!"

And danger signals, never to be forgotten. That day of the bulldog scare. The grinning beast, lunging, ready to grab at the colt's throat, to hang on with his bulldog grip. But the mare's neigh—short, sharp, shrill—crying more plainly than any words, "Danger! Come!" And the little colt bolting for his mother, feeling safe and unafraid in her shadow.

The mare teaches more than alarms. In flytime she hovers over her colt, whisking the biting insects away with her fly-switch tail. By and by the colt learns the trick of it, sidling up to her just so—head to tail—letting her shoo the buzzing, whiny things away. A swish, and they're gone.

If only mares could school humans, too! If only they could gentle humans in the kind and homely things to do. Small ways, folkways that horses like. Take the bit for example. Take it on a cold day. The icy feel of it. How would you like it thrust into your mouth—the cold steel on the warm tongue? Two minutes will warm it. Your hands or your breath can do it.

110

Do you like having your nose stroked? Most horses dislike it, too. Some will tolerate it, a few may enjoy it, but most of them jerk away in distaste, as if their dignity had been offended.

If you can't resist the normal impulse of wanting to touch the horse's velvety nose, offer him the flat of your hand. Let him come sniffing and scenting to you until the feelers of his muzzle tickle your palm. He may even lick the salt of your hand with his big washcloth tongue. In that little moment you have passed the test. You have been accepted.

To most horses the sudden tightening of the girth strap is like the pinching of a vise. Why make it sudden? Why not do it by notches? Easy on the first pull, proffering a wisp of hay to keep his mind and his grinders busy. Now check the bridle or the stirrups and then come back to the buckling. Another notch, another little handout of hay, and soon the girth is as snug as a hoop around a barrel. All this has been accomplished without ears flattened or teeth bared.

Have you seen riders, as they mount, fling their bodies into the saddle, coming down on the horse's back like a sack of potatoes? It is enough to make him jump out of his hide. Some mounts do take a sudden lunge, almost unseating the clumsy rider.

A good horseman mounts lightly, easing himself into the saddle with no shock at all to the horse. Always he avoids startling the high-strung creature. In grooming, in stable care, in all his horse-keeping he works calmly, talks calmly, with never a hustle or bustle. A jerky, head-shy horse is often telltale evidence of an awkward master.

Ever try to walk or run with a stone in your shoe and with a load on your back besides? Horses get stone bruises and corns just as people do. Before and after you ride, remove any little stones imbedded in your horse's feet. He'll feel good, light and airy as any ballet dancer.

When the years pile up on your horse and his teeth wear down and his ribs begin to show, pamper him a little. Try grinding his oats each day and watch him clean up his feed. He'll lose his gaunt look and someone's bound to say, "Got a new horse there, haven't you?"

About this matter of sugaring your horse—don't, for his sake. A horse with a sweet tooth generally turns into a nipper, and sooner or later he is apt to bite the hand that sugars him. Then punishment must be dealt swiftly. One way to avoid the need for punishment is never to give your horse any sugar. If horses could school their masters, the wise ones would say, "Sugar? No, thank you! Save it for your guests who come to tea."

Some trainers believe in breaking a colt, some in gentling him. Breaking is the quick way, gentling the sure way. A circus trainer once received a string of so-called well-broken horses, and at once he saw fear and hatred in their eyes. He might have refused to train them, but their distrust was a challenge.

Before teaching any tricks, he had to start from the beginning, trying to change their opinion of man. For days he took them into the ring during lesson time and just talked to them, letting his voice go up and down the scale as if he were chatting with old cronies. Gradually the horses began to gather around, forking their ears this way and that. "They seemed to like the sound of human voices," the trainer said. "Just because the horse is a dumb animal is no reason for the trainer to be."

Another horseman I know soothes his horses with radio music. It keeps the fractious colt from kicking, he says, and the lonely weanling from crying. One Christmas morning, as I walked into his stable, it was like coming on a nativity scene. High and clear through the air came the song, "Away in a manger, no place for a bed. . . ." And to the rhythm of this gentle melody the horses were munching their sweet-smelling hay and the winter sun was streaming through the open door and a fuzzy colt was lying drowsy and warm in a little nest of straw. Such peace and contentment filled the stable that a mere human seemed an intruder.

As I went crunching away in the snow, I had no words big enough for the peace and the good feeling, but suddenly a high joyous whinny floated out over the half-door. It said all I wanted to say—Merry Christmas!